Helping Children with *Autism* to *Learn*

Edited by Stuart Powell

David Fulton Publishers
London

Note:

Throughout this book pseudonyms are used to protect confidentiality. Where real names are used permission has been given.

David Fulton Publishers Ltd
Ormond House, 26–27 Boswell Street, London WC1N 3JD.
www.fultonbooks.co.uk

First published in Great Britain by David Fulton Publishers 2000

Note: The right of Stuart Powell to be identified as the editor of this work has been asserted by him in accordance with the Copyright, Designs and Patents Act 1988.

British Library Cataloguing in Publication Data
A catalogue record for this book is available from the British Library

ISBN 1–85346–637–9

Typeset by Elite Typesetting Techniques, Eastleigh, Hampshire
Printed in Great Britain by The Cromwell Press Ltd, Trowbridge, Wilts.

Contents

Preface

This book considers how individuals with autism can be enabled to learn through specific approaches to teaching that fall within the context of a broadly consensual view of the nature of autism. The book draws together understandings of how children with autism think and learn and the implications for those who aim to teach them. It is important to note at the outset that 'teach' is used here in its informal as well as formal sense – i.e. including parents and carers as well as teachers. The book aims to offer insights into the reasons behind autistic ways of learning and behaving and give guidance about appropriate ways of responding.

The theme of the book is that in autism the very nature of learning is distinctive and that therefore those involved in the care and education of individuals with autism need to begin by trying to understand the child's perspective on any potential learning and teaching situation. This is not as easy as it might seem because that perspective does not follow the template of a 'normally developing' understanding of what it is to learn and what it is to teach. Understanding on the part of the adult therefore requires some fundamental re-assessing of what is happening whenever the child is faced with an experience that is in any sense new to him/her. The contributing authors show how such re-assessing can take place within their various areas of interest.

The premise underlying the book is that while parents and teachers can benefit from guidance as to how best to proceed in caring for and educating individuals with autism, that guidance needs to incorporate an increase in understanding rather than simply an instruction in skills. If they are to be truly effective, those caring for individuals with autism need insight into *why* they need to approach their task in a particular way and *how* some skills and strategies become useful in autism.

Stuart Powell
University of Hertfordshire
May 2000

Notes on Contributing Authors

MIKAEL HEIMANN is an Associate Professor in the Department of Psychology, Göteborg University, Sweden. A licensed psychologist and psychotherapist, Dr Heimann's research interests include infancy, autism, and the language development of, and computer-aided instruction for children with disabilitities.

FLO LONGHORN has worked in the field of education in the UK, USA and Europe since 1970, with particular emphasis on special education, including expertise in severe and profound disabilities, challenging behaviour and special needs adult education. She has held senior management posts in education, including headships of special needs schools in the UK, and provides special needs consulting in the UK and abroad, in the private and public sectors. For more than two years she was a consultant and trainer at the State Neuro-Psychiatrique Hospital, Ettelbruck, Luxembourg. Currently Flo Longhorn is Principal Consultant in Special Needs and Director of Catalyst Education Resources Ltd, based in Luxembourg and the UK, as well as an Associate Tutor at the Special Education Centre of Westminster College, Oxford. She has published nine books in the area of special education and contributed chapters to several others, and in addition has developed distance learning materials for University of Manchester.

ELIZABETH NEWSON is Consultant in Developmental Psychology to the Early Years Diagnostic Centre, Nottingham, and formerly directed (with John Newson) the Child Development Research Unit at the University of Nottingham, where she held a Chair of Developmental Psychology. Their long-term research on parents' child-rearing methods and outcomes, focusing on both 'ordinary' children and those with special needs, led on to the founding of Sutherland House School and to a series of research projects on autism and intervention, including recent work on interventions with two-year-olds and on differential diagnosis in the pervasive developmental disorders. Professor Newson has always been concerned to establish a 'language of partnership' between children, parents and the professionals who serve them.

MELANIE NIND is Senior Lecturer at the Open University. She has worked as a teacher of children and adults with learning difficulties and autism in a range of school and college contexts. Dr Nind's research is primarily in the area of communication development and she has written extensively on the topic of Intensive Interaction.

THEO PEETERS is a neurolinguist who, after a year internship at TEACCH, founded the Opleidingscentrum Autisme (Center for Training in Autism) in Belgium in l981. Since then, he and his team have been responsible for seminars, workshops and practical training in most European countries and also outside Europe. His Center continues to be affiliated with TEACCH. He has published six books on autism, translated into several languages, two of them in English.

STUART POWELL has worked in mainstream and special school settings both as a class teacher and as a head teacher. In the latter part of his career he has worked as a teacher educator and currently holds posts related to the provision of research degree training at the University of Hertfordshire where he is Professor of Educational Psychology. Professor Powell is Director of the Centre for Autism Studies based at that University. Professor Powell has researched and published widely in the fields of autism, special needs education and critical thinking.

HARRY PROCTER is a consultant clinical psychologist, registered psychotherapist and Head of the Department of Clinical Psychology for children and adolescents in the Somerset Partnership NHS trust. He has developed an approach for working with mental health problems and disabilities based on Kelly's personal construct psychology and has written a series of papers elaborating this approach for adult and child populations. Dr Procter teaches on the MSc course in family therapy and systemic practice at the University of Bristol.

WENDY PREVEZER is a qualified speech and language therapist, and is also a musician. Since 1986 she has combined these two roles in a 'music specialist' post at Sutherland House School in Nottingham, for children with autism. She remains involved with the school on a part-time and consultancy basis, continuing to use and develop the approach known as Musical Interaction. She continued to work part-time for Nottingham's speech and language therapy department until 1997, where she completed a project applying and evaluating the principles of Musical Interaction in a broader context. Currently she runs music sessions with various individuals and groups of children in Nottingham, both with and without special needs, specialising in using music to facilitate social and communication skills. She also runs courses and workshops throughout the country on using musical activities in an interactive approach, and the particular needs of children with autism.

TOMAS TJUS is a lecturer and clinical instructor in the Department of Psychology, Göteborg University, Sweden. A licensed psychologist and psychotherapist, Dr Tjus's research interests include developmental psychopathology and the language development of, and computer-aided instruction for, children with disabilities.

Chapter One

Learning about Life Asocially: The Autistic Perspective on Education

Stuart Powell

Introduction

The title of this book points deliberately to a specific stance with regard to the education of children with autism. It suggests that in autism, perhaps more than in any other context, the very nature of teaching and learning needs a special kind of scrutiny. There is an underlying premise here that what can usually be assumed when anyone engages in trying to teach something to someone else cannot be assumed in autism. The individual with autism needs help to learn. For example, it is not enough to ask from the singular perspective of the teacher, 'How can I motivate this child to learn?' Rather the question needs to be, 'How can I help this child learn to be motivated?' Clearly, to get to a position where an answer to this latter question can be reached there first needs to be some understanding of what is habitually regarded, in this instance, as 'being motivated' and more generally as the process of teaching and learning. Following this there needs to be some consideration of what effect the autism will have on that way of being and that process. In autism effective teaching can only be realised by an initial consideration of the individual's way of learning and its effects on whatever the teacher might plan to do. Education in autism needs to be pursued from the child's perspective.

In this introductory chapter I try to justify the stance described above and the implied way of operating by considering the relationship between *autism, meaning* and *self* and subsequent implications for those engaged in trying to help children with autism to learn. In doing this I draw on the writings of others (e.g. Peeters 1997) and make use of some speculative findings (e.g. Luckett, unpublished). I am, therefore, offering <u>an</u> account rather than stating established facts. It is my hope that readers will find this account useful when considering the ideas and practices of the contributing authors. It is not my intention here to suggest any consensual view of the nature of autism nor indeed to include reference to competing theories (for a review of various theoretical approaches to autism see Powell 1999).

Meaning

This section on meaning is influenced by *Autism: from theoretical understanding to educational intervention* by Theo Peeters (Peeters 1997; and Chapter 2 of this book).

Making meaning and learning meaning

Central to the way in which most of us perceive, and act upon, the world around us is our inclination to make meaning of that world. When things are presented to us meaningfully they are easier to understand and remember than when they are presented meaninglessly. Indeed, if things seem meaningless then to understand and remember them effectively we may strive to make them meaningful by imposing a meaning of our own. For example, one way to memorise a random selection of words is to create a meaningful story that incorporates them, even if that story has to be implausible and bizarre in order to incorporate them all.

Meaning is central to our socially constructed way of living. Objects and events have meaning or are given meaning and this enables us to manage our world and learn within it. Yet in a different culture acceptable meanings might differ. Words, gestures, actions, tolerances, objects: all differ in what they mean in relation to the specific cultural context in which they are found. While we might not recognise it overtly, what things mean is largely a matter of what we have learnt that they mean. That learning, of course, is in turn largely informal and intuitive. The young girl gets to know what her father thinks about eating meat because of what he says and what he does, the kinds of expression that he makes when he eats meat (or avoids it) and so on. Other episodes of others' reactions to meat eating are learning experiences that lead to an understanding on the part of the girl about the meaning of meat eating. No direct teaching need go on here (though it might, and indeed it may include scientific understandings about proteins etc.) but the learning is significant and long lasting nonetheless. Meat eating is valued and treated differently in different cultures and subcultures – its meaning is not consistent. So, meaning is learnt in a pervasive, implicit and social way within the confines of a particular context. To a very large extent things mean what people agree that they will mean. Because of constraints on space and the need to focus sharply on an autistic perspective on the world I am sidestepping some significant philosophical and epistemological issues here (tackled elsewhere, e.g. Bruner 1990) and some issues within the literature on autism which relate to the perception and learning of meaning (e.g. Frith and Happe 1994). Whatever issues surrounding this topic remain unresolved it may well be that those with experience of working with individuals with autism recognise that here some of the aspects of the learning of meaning are dysfunctional. Indeed, those with autism are often described as being outside of the culture in which they live, as not accessing the kinds of beliefs, understandings and skills that are typically taken for granted as accepted within a particular society. Perhaps the most obvious instance of dysfunction in relation to the example in the previous paragraph is the potential for learning from 'kinds of expression'. Children with autism find it difficult to detect the meaning of what is being said from the clues offered by the expression of the speaker. In this sense learning of meaning does not occur naturally in autism. This difficulty in learning about what things mean in the way that is assumed by the non-autistic results in any 'meaning' that *is* achieved remaining idiosyncratic (and thus limited in usefulness) and rigid (unlikely to change as new experiences are encountered). The child with autism who wears a particular hat whenever he goes to the shops but never when he goes anywhere else is displaying a learnt preference indicating that the hat has a particular meaning, which relates in this instance to shopping. However, the meaning is for him alone, it is not shared by others.

Implications of the lack of use of meaning

Reliance on rote memory

Lack of ability to use meaning to organise the experiences of the world, and in particular the social world, is likely to increase the load on memory in that the child with autism cannot code lots of information within a meaningful structure. A whole mass of new information can be made manageable by the child without autism because it can be understood as a structure with clear connections; yet that same information can remain disconnected and therefore unmanageable to the child with autism. So, for example, a boy without autism is able to cope with a trip to a new shopping centre because the buildings where goods are sold are understood as shops within which the functions of display cases and shop assistants and the roles of other customers are all readily understood. This non-autistic boy has an expectation that several shops will be visited and refreshments will be taken: for him a shopping trip is a meaningful event. However, in the same scenario the child with autism is faced with a bewildering set of confusing stimuli. Nothing makes sense because understandings of purposes, functions, roles and time constraints have not been learnt. If the child does not have meaning to help him then he will have to rely on rote memory all the time and subsequently will be less efficient at remembering and less flexible in coping with new and changing experiences. The example used here is based on a social event. But the same principles apply in the context of the learning of academic material. New information about Victorian England can be understood when existing concepts about invention, industry, poverty, diet, fashions and games enable the learner to organise the new information in meaningful ways. When children understand about playing games then they are able to understand the nature of 'games playing' in Victorian times even if the games themselves are totally new to them.

Difficulties with prediction

When a child learns the meaning of something then it becomes possible for her to begin to estimate on the basis of that meaning. Once she has a conception of 'ball' that includes 'bouncing' then she can predict that a ball will bounce once dropped (and later come to more sophisticated estimations of height of bounce in relation to consistencies of ball and surface and to velocity of throw etc.). If the child can solve, for example, tasks involving partially hidden figures she is showing evidence that she can go beyond the information that is present and determine what the whole of the shape may be on the basis of what she can see. Here she estimates meaning from the clues that are available to her. Being able to successfully complete a partially hidden figure indicates one of the most useful aspects of meaning – its potential to enable prediction. Meaning allows us to understand what the rest of something is like, what something will be like when something else changes it, what something will be like in the future.

Now again, where children without autism typically display the ability to go beyond the information that is given to them, for example to predict, pretend, infer and extrapolate, those with autism find it difficult to do these things. Children with autism will perform less well than children of similar mental age on tasks such as the partially hidden figures task mentioned above. There is a sense in which the understanding of those with autism remains at the level of the perceptual – it is literal and objective. In some contexts literality and objectivity are useful dimensions to thinking; for example, in proof reading text or in working through particular mathematical algorithms. But in other contexts these dimensions are less useful and in some cases can be deleterious to problem-solving; for example in analysing poetry or using humourous analogies to make a point (see Chapter 8). The ability to move away from the literal and the objective to an understanding that things can have meaning beyond what is perceptually available is extremely useful. It is an ability that underpins much of the non-autistic way of thinking and learning yet one that is largely inaccessible for those with autism.

Difficulties in making connections

It is the meaningfulness of things that enables us to make connections between different events. If 'understandings' were to remain at the level of the perceptual, at a literal/objective level, then they would remain isolated in our minds. For example, it is because I know something of the meaning of a violent act that I am able to make connections between a fight in the playground, racial hatred, genocide, the Thirty Years War and violent crime on the streets. Not that these things are the same, of course, but it is meaning that enables me to begin to connect them together in an understanding of how they are similar and how they are different. Without these kinds of meanings connections will always remain simplistic, direct and inflexible and, again, this seems to be the case in autism.

Difficulties with categorisation

Young children without autism are driven to make sense of the world. Part of this drive involves the need to categorise. Certainly they make mistakes of categorisation – for example, calling all four-legged furry things dogs regardless of whether they might, in fact, be cats or something else – but they learn the rules by which categorisation takes place. And in this learning they seem to be influenced intuitively by meaning rather than perception. They learn that while things might look the same or sound the same or feel the same they fall into categories that mean what 'we' have all agreed they will mean. So a donkey is not a horse even though it looks like one, feels like one, smells a bit like one and acts much the same as one. Also, children learn about the vagaries of commonplace descriptions of categories of things. They learn, for example, that a coat might also be described as an anorak or a jacket.

In autism, however, the situation described above is reversed. Here children have a tendency to be influenced by perception rather than meaning. This tendency is exemplified by Peeters (1997) when he describes a boy called Thomas who gave names to things that were the same but which didn't look exactly alike. He had different bicycles which he called: 'bicycle', 'wheels in the mud', 'wheels in the grass', 'feet on the pedals'. At one level this may sound creative but he could not understand what his parents were saying to him if they said, 'get on your bicycle' if his 'feet on the pedals' happened to be in front of him.

In autism, perceptually-based rather than meaning-based development leads inevitably to a lack of understanding of socially accepted categorisations. So a child with autism might have real difficulties in accepting that the different things in front of him are conceptually bound within a collective notion of 'bicycle'. Similarly another child might have difficulties in accepting that what she knows as her jacket might equally well be referred to as an anorak or a coat. Her understanding is locked in to the one case that she has come to understand as relating to the label 'jacket'.

Self

In this section the relationship between the development of meaning and sense of self in autism is explored. This exploration is of a psychological kind; there is no intention here to make allusion to the moral, legal or sociological selfhood of individuals with autism. The need to recognise qualities in these respects is returned to at the end of the chapter.

Levels of self in autism

Neisser (1988) has described levels of self: the ecological, interpersonal, conceptual, temporally extended and finally private self. This way of conceptualising self is useful for my purposes because it enables a way of describing self in autism as a matter of partial development. Clearly it would not be correct to say that individuals with autism have no sense of self because we know, for example, that they can recognise themselves in a mirror (provided they are above 18 months mental age). On the other hand individuals with autism do seem to have difficulties in developing a sense of self in relation to others in the world and in particular in relation to the ever-shifting patterns of social happenings. In terms of Neisser's model then it seems that the ecological self may well develop in autism. For example, children with autism often seem to be very aware of where they are in space, they are very good at squeezing through small spaces and knowing where they will and will not fit. But their difficulties begin at the level of the interpersonal self.

The interpersonal self

Functions of the interpersonal self

It is the interpersonal self, in Neisser's model, that enables individuals to know that they are having experiences which relate in some way to the experiences of others. For example, the student without autism who sits in a lecture listening to the teacher knows that the words spoken are what he is hearing and that others can hear them too. He also knows, at some level, that those words will be affecting others differently according to the prior knowledge and experience that they bring to the situation. It is this interpersonal self together with the conceptual self that enables individuals to begin to code events as part of a personal dimension. The student makes sense of the lecture, or not, according to how it affects him as a person in relation to others – as someone with more or less knowledge and experience and with certain intentions and not others. In this example the student makes more of the lecture than would be involved by a simple encoding of the words spoken. The event becomes meaningful because he is able to relate what he hears to what he already knows and to what he thinks he will be able to do with the new knowledge, i.e. how it affects *him* and what *he* knows.

Again, the difficulty in autism becomes apparent in the breakdown of the normal synergy between meaning, social mediation and self. The student with autism has difficulty in picking up the socially conveyed meanings (some of which will be extremely subtle and implied) and difficulty in relating his own understanding to that of others. The knowledge that he does pick up in this kind of scenario will tend to be factual, disconnected and impersonal.

Implications of difficulties in developing an interpersonal self

If, as I suggest, there are difficulties in developing an interpersonal self in autism, and beyond to a conceptual self, then the individual with autism is in a position where events are experienced but at a perceptual level, non-subjectively. In a sense the individual is operating within the ecological level of Neisser's model and is thus acting according to an objective reality that is not mediated by any social implicatures or socially defined meanings.

Such difficulties will mean that there will be problems in learning through social interactions about the self and others as 'mental agents'. In short, the non-autistic learn that they and others have attitudes and beliefs and, furthermore, learn to act according to these things rather than according to 'objective reality'. (They may of course act contrary to prevalent, accepted attitudes but this would be for purposes of rebellion or rejection rather than unknowingly.) This early learning leads to the later, 'sophisticated' understanding that people's actions and behaviours relate as much to their attitudes as to any sense of objective fact. For example, one can understand that people behave towards those of a different culture and/or colour of skin because of the attitudes they hold towards different cultures and skin colours rather than to any 'objective facts' about these things. All of this learning will be impaired in autism.

Experiencing self

Sense of agency

One reason for having a self in psychological terms is that the 'I' becomes a unified centre of experience with a past and a future, capable of learning from the first to meet the needs of the second. In other words, the 'I' develops into an experiencing self with a very real sense of experiencing the world from the inside rather than from a detached or 'third party' position (Powell and Jordan 1993).

One of the key ways in which this is apparent is in the way in which people sense that they act on the world around them. People know when they are responsible for the changes in their experience as opposed to when these happen as the result of something or somebody else. It is this sense of responsibility which makes these experiences their own. Russell (1996) points out that there can be no conception of that which 'I know' or 'I believe' or 'I perceive', or indeed that these mental states are 'my own', unless 'I am somebody who wills' (p.179).

In autism it seems that awareness of being an 'I who wills' is somehow impaired and therefore the conceptions of 'I knowing' and 'I believing' and 'I perceiving' are consequently difficult.

Lack of an experiencing self

We need to consider the difficulty an individual might find herself in if she did *not* have an experiencing self in this sense: one of the things she might have trouble with understanding is intentional behaviour. If she did not have a sense of her own agency, of her causing effects both in the environment at large and within herself, then it would come as no surprise if she failed to learn about herself and others as individual centres of attitudes, beliefs and intentions in the typical way. In fact, if an individual was in that position then she would have to theorise about minds in order to figure out why others behave in the ways that they do. This kind of theorising would replace the intuitive understandings of how other people 'must' be thinking and feeling in given situations. The girl might need to work out, at the level of theory, what the child in the picture story is thinking and feeling as the wind blows her kite away. Equally if she had trouble grasping the subjective nature of attitudes, she might assume that the world as it appears to her is 'just the way it is' for everyone else. It seems that this may be the position of children with autism. If this is the case then it goes some way to explaining why they present as 'locked in their own world', why they are literal and necessarily rigid in their thinking.

A difference in the way experience feels in autism

Luckett *et al.* (unpublished) have tried to find out if children with autism have a weaker understanding of the personal nature of attitudes and intentions by getting them to contrast their attitudes with those of others in ambiguous situations. They adapted a study used with preschoolers by Flavell *et al.* (1990). Most of the children with autism seemed to understand that when someone pulled a disgusted face it meant that a particular drink tasted bad. However, once they themselves had tasted the drink and found that they liked it, they tended to say that the first person must also have liked it. Effectively, they ignored the earlier evidence. Since some of these children were able to pass a standard false belief test, it seems that their difficulty was not with understanding the representational nature of mental states. Instead, it may be that these children did not understand the personal, subjective nature of likes and dislikes; they assumed that the drink was either good or bad tasting *full stop*. They were having difficulty in understanding that their attitudes, indeed their liking, could differ from someone else's. In a sense these children were assuming a wholly objective stance to the world where subjectivity of experience played no part. If this is so, then it points to a difference in the way experience feels for those with autism. In another task children were asked to cooperate with the experimenter in playing a game involving putting down 'stepping stones' (sheets of paper) to enable their partner (the experimenter) to cross the room. It was clear that some children with autism (with quite high verbal mental ages) found it difficult to relate their own sense of agency to their partner's needs and intentions.

Difficulty in learning about social shared meaning is central to the autistic way of thinking and is rooted in the particular way experience feels in autism. Here the experiencing self does not include the 'I am somebody who wills' and therefore the delicate balance between intention to act within any social context and awareness that any resulting act will necessarily involve interpersonal relatedness will be disrupted. The learning of social shared meaning is dependent on that balance being maintained – and so in autism the learning that does go on is distinctive in being asocial, non-subjective and unconnected.

Implications for teaching

If we can accept that there are qualitative differences in autistic thinking, and perhaps that some of these are profound and pervasive, then the following implications arise for teachers and carers.

Understanding the autistic perspective

To see the world from an autistic perspective is as unnatural for the non-autistic as it is for those with autism to understand the 'normal' social world. It requires suspension of the assumptions upon which we normally operate. We cannot assume that learners will attend to contextual features when interpreting what people mean by what they say and what they do. For example, the child with autism may not be able to identify what a simple wave is meant to convey ('hello', 'goodbye', 'I need attention') from the context in which it is made even though that child can wave and can do so appropriately when cued. Further, we cannot assume that the child with autism will understand or be able to operate on the basis that how one feels about something is not necessarily how everyone else feels about it.

Clearly it is challenging to try to suspend the very basis for one's own behaviours and beliefs when trying to interpret the behaviour of the child with autism in the classroom. But there is a need to recognise that this is the mirror image of the challenge that faces the individual with autism in trying to cope with the non-autistic world. Taking an autistic perspective means thinking through the curriculum and its delivery from the perspective of someone for whom meaning remains idiosyncratic and where the social conveyancing of knowledge and skills does not function effectively.

Learning about learning

There is a need to work to an agenda about learning what learning *is* as well as to the learning of 'material'. Certainly the teacher can find ways of enabling children with autism to memorise facts. But those same children will not necessarily realise that what they are experiencing may relate to prior experiences, that these particular facts relate to others that they already 'know'. They will not automatically realise that what they are doing now may have relevance for what they may do later. Autistic learning is of a disconnected kind and therefore pupils with autism need to be shown what connections *are* as well as what the specific connections are within the particular learning experience with which they are engaged. They will need visual structure (picture cards, photographs, video) that makes overt the connections between different aspects of their learning and between what they learn and what they can do. They may also benefit from a kind of micro-teaching where what they have learnt can be made apparent by re-running a learning event (involving themselves) on video and having their attention drawn to its significance *for them*.

Focus on memory

From what has been suggested earlier in this chapter it is clear that the role of memory in autistic learning is distinctive. Particular attention needs to be paid therefore to the kinds of memory burdens that are imposed on children with autism in their day-to-day lives and in particular aspects of their schooling. Expectations in this respect should not be based on assumptions derived from the teacher's own experience of how to remember. Teachers need to recognise the effects of what they are doing when they make use of particular teaching strategies and broad educational approaches that involve memory processing. For example, a strategy that resolves an inability to remember in the short term (e.g. carrying a picture depicting the task for the duration of the activity) may create a new kind of dependency (e.g. the child becomes dependent on someone else providing a picture to enable task completion). Here the teacher needs to remain aware of the difficulties experienced by the child at a psychological as well as at a behavioural level. The teacher also needs to be able to identify inherent possibilities within the task situation for the child to learn about remembering as well as to function effectively. So in the example above it might be possible for the child to begin to choose the picture for herself (from a limited selection) that will enable her to complete the task. Such an act of choosing would mean that the child is beginning to take control over the mechanics of her own learning. In this way she is learning about strategies for remembering and is in a position where she can begin to learn about how and when to employ them.

Focus on self

Again, the role of self in learning in autism may be distinctive. Certainly, what can be assumed with the non-autistic in this respect cannot necessarily be assumed with the autistic. Teachers may therefore need to pay specific attention to the way in which the child with autism's sense of self operates within the learning and teaching situation. The child's attention may usefully be focused on her own actions rather than on the products of that action. For example, in autism it may be important for the teacher to draw the child's attention to the fact that she *is* drawing with a crayon and then that she *has* drawn rather than attending solely to the drawing itself. Praising the qualities in a drawing diminishes in meaningfulness if the child is not fully aware of her own sense of agency and therefore ownership in relation to that drawing.

Focus on meaning

The implications for the psychology of the child with autism in relation to any lack of ability to make use of meaning have been outlined earlier in this chapter. For the teacher this presents a very particular set of challenges. The normally accepted conventions whereby meaning can be best conveyed with high levels of social mediation may not apply; thus children may learn more effectively in asocial contexts, for example such as those involving information technology. Similarly, wherever meaning is assumed the child with autism will be disadvantaged, for example in the unthinking use of humour to emphasise a point (see Chapter 8 for a description of a thoughtful way to use humour). The child with autism may not be proactive in organising the world in such a way as to make it meaningful and therefore manageable. This may result in teachers doing that kind of organising for the child, for example by marking out physical spaces in such a way as to indicate different purposes. In all of this the fundamental issue is that education is concerned with the communication of meaning and specifically meaning which is commonly accepted and commonly perceived as being worthy. Children with autism are outside of these, often tacit, agreements. This means that teachers need to challenge fundamental assumptions about what things mean, how values are placed on them and how that meaning can effectively be conveyed. This challenge needs to extend, for example, from the social meaning of events such as school assembly to the meaning of numbers and their addition and subtraction.

Teaching towards increased independence

One of the difficulties of working with children with autism is that they may, albeit unintentionally, draw the teacher into an autistic style of teaching in which accurate cues are readily provided in order to trigger memory for disconnected bits of knowledge and disparate skills. Clearly what is needed is a kind of teaching that leads to increasing independence for the child rather than increasing dependency of the child on the teacher to provide the right cues. So, ways need to be found of developing 'independent working' using, for example, visual schedules, aides-memoire and so on. There is a need to address the fundamental issue of how the thinking of these children can be made more effective, always accepting that teachers need to address this issue at the level at which the children are able to operate. It cannot be enough to talk only of containment (of difficult behaviours) and of increasing functional ability (of being able to cope in specified situations). Children with autism are entitled to more than these things. They may need to be helped to learn and that learning may need to start at very functional levels, but the ultimate aim must be to increase an individual's abilities to think and act independently. In the chapters that follow the various contributing authors try to set out ways in which independent thinking can be achieved in autism.

Conclusion

In this chapter I have described a sense in which individuals with autism are outside of the culture. I mean this, of course, in a psychological sense only. When they are able to engage in learning it may seem as if they are looking in from the outside and trying to work out what it is that the rest are all doing. In this respect the learning that they achieve will inevitably be the result of considerable effort on their part and their contribution to the process of learning should never be underestimated. But I am suggesting more than that we should be sympathetic to the plight of the autistic. I am arguing for a careful structuring of how educationists respond to autism according to a best understanding of how things are for the individuals concerned. This involves respecting their position as well as striving to understand it. To these ends I use the words of Jim Sinclair (1992) to set the scene for what follows in the subsequent chapters of this book.

> But my personhood is intact. My selfhood is undamaged. I find value and meaning in life, and I have no wish to be cured of being myself. Grant me the dignity of meeting me on my own terms... Recognise that we are equally alien to each other, that my ways of being are not merely damaged versions of yours. Question your assumptions. Define your terms. Work with me to build bridges between us.

Let me take some of the key phrases from this quote in turn. The underlinings below are mine not Sinclair's.

- 'I find <u>value and meaning</u> in life, and I have no wish to be cured of being myself.' It is all too easy to define value and meaning in our own terms and in so doing to fail to recognise that what we value is not necessarily universally valued. Definitions of everything from *learning* to *friendship* to what counts as a *leisure activity* are culturally bound. Teachers should not hold back from trying to make things better for the individual but do need to challenge accepted notions of what counts as 'better'.
- 'Grant me the dignity of meeting me on my own terms... Recognise that we are equally alien to each other, that <u>my ways of being are not merely damaged versions of yours</u>.' What is required here is that we respect a difference rather than seek to establish a commonality. Education should be about celebrating diversity. While there may be different ways of developing none is particularly 'right' or 'wrong'. But all ways of developing will have implications for ways of learning and responsiveness to teaching.
- 'Question your <u>assumptions</u>.' In daily life assumptions based on particular cultural expectations are made continuously. Similarly, in formal teaching situations, assumptions are made that are based on a template of what counts as learning and are based on a particular view of the pupil as a learner (i.e. as someone actively trying to make sense of the world). In autism both of these assumptions do not hold true and therefore for teachers to base what they do upon them is unlikely to lead to effective teaching.
- '<u>Define your terms</u>.' Teachers need to define for those with autism just what it is that they really mean and not confuse them by hiding agenda and purpose behind the usual barrage of implication and shared complicity. This requires them to redefine notions of teaching and learning. It is not always easy to let go of accepted practices but in autism it seems essential. There is a need to reassess what is put into a curriculum as well as the kinds of teaching approaches adopted.
- 'Work with me to <u>build bridges</u> between us.' In autism it is all too easy to find oneself working against the grain. There is a need to try to reconceptualise teaching and learning in autism as a matter of the teacher learning about how the pupil can learn. In autism the teacher needs to become a learner first, needs to re-examine her own intuitive responses in any teaching and learning situation and accept the need to join with the pupil and start from where that pupil *is* rather than from where she would like him or her to be.

Acknowledgement

I am grateful for the help of Tim Luckett and Rona Tutt, both of whom made very useful comments on early drafts of this chapter.

References

Bruner, J. S. (1990) *Acts of Meaning*. Harvard: Harvard University Press.

Flavell, J. H., Flavell, E. R., Green, F. L. and Moses, L. J. (1990) 'Young children's understanding of fact beliefs versus value beliefs', *Child Development* **61**, 915–28.

Frith, U. and Happe, F. (1994) 'Autism – beyond theory of mind', *Cognition* **50**, 115–32.

Luckett, T., Powell, S. D., Messer, D. J., Thornton, M. E. and Schulz, J. (unpublished) Agency and intention: Understanding of self and other in autism.

Neisser, U. (1988) 'Five kinds of self knowledge', *Philosophical Psychology* **1**, 35–59.

Peeters, T. (1997) *Autism: from theoretical understanding to educational intervention*. London: Whurr Publishers.

Powell, S. D. (1999) 'Autism', in Messer, D. and Millar, S. (eds) *Developmental Psychology*. Cambridge: Cambridge University Press.

Powell, S. D. and Jordan, R. R. (1993) 'Being subjective about autistic thinking and learning to learn', *Educational Psychology* **13** (3+4), 359–70.

Russell, J. (1996) *Agency: Its Role in Mental Development*. London: Erlbaum.

Sinclair, J. (1992) 'Bridging the gaps: an inside-out view of autism' in Schopler, E. and Mesibov, G. (eds) *High Functioning Individuals with Autism*. New York: Plenum Press.

Chapter Two

The Language of Objects

Theo Peeters

Introduction

It was 30 years ago and one of my first experiences with a child with autism. Donald had a severe developmental delay as well as autism. I had prepared such a beautiful activity with his bag. After the first minute of this beautiful activity he developed a temper tantrum. I, of course, feared he did not like me… Why not?

I found out that he associated this bag with going home. When I gave him his bag he thought I was telling him: 'It is time to go home.' After one minute he found out that I had been lying to him, because he had to stay for my beautiful exercise. I learned a lot from this stupid mistake. I learned that objects can speak and it seems to me now that this is a good first lesson for anyone involved in communication processes in autism.

Recently, during a practical training session, I saw one of the participants make a similar mistake. At the end of the day's program she helped Ronaldo to put on his shoes. Ten minutes later Ronaldo was still in the free time area not knowing what had happened to him: this adult had 'told' him to go home and here he still was waiting. He started to hit himself very hard. The participant was left wondering why Ronaldo had this challenging behaviour. One of the very important aspects professionals have to learn is that objects may have a communication value for persons with autism.

One of the other aspects to learn is that there are many different languages in the use of objects, just as in the use of words. For the three-dimensional object we drink from we have the word glass; we have the word *verre, bicchiere, pohar, vaso, becher, potere* and so on. But glasses may have different forms, colours, textures, smells, and for a person with autism without an internal concept of 'glass' they may represent a world of differences.

Judy had learned to associate a plate with eating. She seemed so proud and happy about this understanding, her first entering into the world of meaning. And then one day when given a plate and sitting at the table she started screaming very loudly: another behaviour problem. In Judy's hyperselective thinking the texture was very important in trying to make sense out of the world. She had learned to recognise how pleasant and meaningful it was to touch a wooden plate, especially if it was followed immediately by something to eat. Yet that special day one unthinking professional had given her a plastic plate as a symbol for time to eat. In almost the only thing Judy really understood of meaning in life she felt terribly cheated and reacted violently.

In training professionals one of the first things to learn is that behaviour problems may be expressions of stress, may in fact be 'pre-communicative' behaviours, desperate attempts at trying to say something for which one still does not have words or other symbols. Our reaction should always be: what is he trying to say through his behaviour? Is not his reaction related to his 'autism thinking'? What has he understood differently? Is it then possible for us to communicate our expectations in an alternative way, at an individualised symbolic level, through written words, or through pictures, or through objects (or through details of objects)?

Symbols of a 'lower' or 'higher' value

There is something strange about the use of objects as a mode of communication, or should I say: there is something strange about our minds. Very often I have found that professionals who want to help non-verbal persons with autism almost automatically think of the use of pictures, as if objects were too low in value. I believe that one of the prices that students with autism have to pay for 'normalisation' is that we all too often aim at the highest possible symbolic level of abstraction for communication and education, not necessarily at the highest level of independence for the students themselves. All too often this seems to be associated with the never explicitly formulated opinion that after all the way in which we (the 'normal') tend to think is the best way, if not the only way, of thinking.

It is important to realise that we also use objects more than we think for communication. I show a watch (it is time to go), I show a glass (let's have a drink), I show the car keys (we have to leave), etc. And the need to have communication at an object level becomes more urgent and necessary when we are stranded in another culture without an orientation manual – which is how Jim Sinclair (1992) describes the experience of having autism.

You are in Flanders and I communicate to you in four different symbolic levels. Which communication level would be easiest for you?
• Spoken message: not printed here, since verbal words are invisible and fugitive.
• Spoken message together with the written message: Wilt ge met me mee komen eten?
• Spoken message together with the picture of a plate.
• Spoken message together with the real plate.

Everyone will tell me that the communication with an object was the easiest one to understand. Yet by a lack of true comprehension we risk not allowing students with autism, with severe communication problems, to have access to very concrete messages at an object level.

Access to the world of symbols equals access to a typically human world

The more we try to imagine how it would be to live with a combination of autism and a profound developmental delay, the more we feel our limits. Philosophers have said that entering the world of meaning is the door to human development. Is it possible that some of our citizens still live in a world without meaning, where a perception is a perception is a perception and nothing else beyond the literal information? Living in such a world may mean that everything seems dominated by coincidence, where one is the victim of things happening without any possibility of anticipation. Such a life would be one without real power over the environment and therefore a resultant dependency on others to structure, guide and protect.

Clearly such citizens (and my suggestion is, of course, that some citizens with autism find themselves in this position) would need our sense of responsibility and care more than anyone else. And it should be clear right from the beginning that we need to adapt our teaching of meaning to their brain functioning, instead of expecting them to adapt to our level of meaning. The strong should adapt to the weaker, not the other way round.

It is well known that we have a left and a right hemisphere and that each half of the brain is specialised in dealing with certain skills, the left specialised in speech production for instance, the right dealing with space. It is a little bit less known that each hemisphere also has its specialised way of dealing with information. The right brain is specialised in perceptual synthesis; the left brain is specialised in conceptual analysis. Gazzaniga (1970) gives a nice and simple example. Here you have an apple and an orange. For the right brain they are alike because both are round. One does not have to go beyond the perception, you see immediately that they are round. The roundness of an apple and an orange does not have to be analysed; it is information speaking for itself. For the left brain an apple and an orange are alike because both of them are fruit. The 'fruit-ness' of an apple and an orange does not speak for itself; it has to be analysed according to meaning. This conceptual information is rather open. Here one has to go beyond the literal perceptual information. Understanding the meaning of speech and of social interaction is essentially the result of the left brain analysis.

Now it seems that persons with autism may treat much communicative and social information with right brain strategies, much longer than one would expect for their developmental ages. Abstracting meaning from social and communicative processes is much more difficult than we suppose and especially in these areas persons with autism seem to be more dominated by their perception than by their analysis of meaning. Therefore we see echo-effects (the literal processing of information) much longer than one would expect for their general developmental level (Happe 1995; Jordan 1996; Peeters 1997). This has far reaching effects for communication and education.

My experience shows that the capacity to abstract meaning (out of our communication and our social interactions) in individuals with autism is less developed than their general developmental level suggests. Two examples will serve to illustrate this notion.

1. I know a six-year-old boy with autism. His name is Tom. He has a general developmental age of two and yet he does not abstract meaning from speech. He cannot analyse the meaning from a drawing. He does not understand what his mother means when she shows him his shoes.

2. I know Kitty, she is an adult with autism with a general developmental age of two and a half. She understands no pictures. When I first met her she did not understand that she was going to eat when the carer showed her a spoon. Instead of understanding the meaning of objects, she strictly associated them with a certain context. Spoons, forks and plates had to stay in the kitchen. When she found a spoon left somewhere in the grass she started crying: the little she understood of the world was turned upside down. Every object seen in a different context could turn into a nightmare for her.

Tom and Kitty do not understand pictures or the meaning of objects beyond their functional value. They will have to learn to understand symbols and then later use them expressively for communication. If we are not conscious of the fact that the capacity of abstraction may be lower than the general developmental age suggests, then we might propose an education at the level of the general developmental age for Tom and for Kitty. This education may well respond to our expectations and dreams, but much less to the real level of understanding of Tom and Kitty.

I will try to formulate the conclusion of this section a little bit differently. Persons with autism are relatively strong in processing information that is: concrete, visible, and in space. Whereas persons with autism are relatively weak in processing information that is: abstract, invisible and in time (i.e. transient, fugitive, temporal). In our traditional (special) education we are used to passing on information in an abstract, invisible, temporal mode (our brains are very good at this). Instead of saying that Tom and Kitty are weak in abstract, invisible and temporal information and that they have to learn to function like us, we will say that Tom and Kitty have strengths that we will use. So we will try to develop a different perspective (a revolutionary one perhaps) on the education for persons with autism and turn our abstract, invisible, temporal messages into concrete, visible and spatial ones. This is the real meaning of integration: where the stronger adapts to the weaker.

Augmentative communication and augmentative education

There was a time when non-verbal children were pushed and pushed towards speech. If speech did not come, then the child could not be helped. Later the insight grew that, after all, speech is just one form of communication (the most abstract, invisible, temporal form). After all, children with difficulties in developing language could learn to communicate if language was supported with concrete and visible forms of communication: pictures, objects. The expression augmentative communication reflects a new insight into the learning of those with autism and in this sense perhaps offers a message of hope. Similarly, there was a time when children with autism were considered as ineducable. Afterwards the insight grew that children with autism were only ineducable if they were asked to adapt to a type of education that did not, in fact address their very real learning needs (was not 'autism specific').

As soon as educationists began to understand that children with autism treated information differently and to propose an education adapted to this different brain functioning it became clear that these children are able to learn more than we ever thought. For some children verbal teaching was supported by two-dimensional symbols (pictures, photos), while for others verbal teaching was supported by objects. In short, teaching became more concrete, visible, spatial. Also, the expression augmentative education reflects this new insight, it is a message full of hope.

We will now further develop this theme of augmentative communication and augmentative education at an object level. Especially, if we think of students with autism at a very young developmental age, the basis of an education consists of two elements: the creation of predictability in space and time, and the injection of feelings of success through independent tasks. Elsewhere (Peeters 1997; Peeters and Gillberg 1999) I have explained the basic principles, so I will only summarise the main points here.

The creation of predictability in space: the language of objects

In a pre-symbolic world there is little or no independence or self-esteem. Persons with very young developmental ages have to learn that this world is one of meaning, that there are meaningful connections between objects and activities or situations. Since these persons seem to have pervasive difficulties in developing flexible thinking and seem to be better talented at making concrete associations teachers will exploit their strengths. I will illustrate what I mean by concrete associations through a few anecdotes.

One child had experienced that after having watched TV it was time for supper. He made a concrete association: TV – then eating. One evening after having watched his programme, father was not home yet. There he was; the whole house was full of information about eating, the table was set, he smelled food, TV was over, but nobody started eating. He felt cheated and developed a temper tantrum. He had done his very best to understand a little about this complicated life, and people did not respect his understanding.

Another boy smiled very happily when he came downstairs from his bedroom. Mother wondered why. He liked his breakfast, yes, he also liked going to school, but she could not understand why he looked so extraordinarily happy. Then, when the school bus came his smile disappeared, in fact it was a struggle to get him on the bus. Was he a 'bad boy' or did he simply understand things differently? As a good detective his mother tried to find the reason for his happiness that changed so suddenly into unhappiness. Then she saw that she had left the folding chair in the corridor, the yellow folding chair that they had taken to the beach last weekend. Now everything became clear. Her boy had made a concrete association between the yellow folding chair and the beach. He had tried to understand the world his own way instead of the way we want.

It is this natural tendency to try to understand the world through making concrete associations that we as carers will use to organise the classroom or the group home, so that the world becomes more predictable. We need to teach our pupils with autism that there is a predictable relationship between spaces and activities and behaviours. We need to make explicit: this is the activity corner: this is where you do school activities, where a learning behaviour is expected, always here, but only here. This is the free time corner: this is where you can let yourself go, no learning or concentration here. This is the domestic area: this is where you eat with the other students and where self-help skills are being taught.

If all these behaviours and activities can be associated with predictable places then life for the pupils is a little bit more under control, then they have gained a bit of power and independence, this may be the beginning of a good feeling about themselves, the first injection of success. My suggestion here is that this success may be generated by our use of the language of objects. For example, the answer to the question 'where do I do things' is given in a concrete visible spatial way.

The creation of predictability in time: the language of objects

One does not see time directly. Time has to be analysed. If we can accept that dealing with abstract, invisible, temporal information may be particularly difficult for children with autism, then clearly dealing with time must be particularly onerous. Time is very abstract, time is invisible and it has a transient quality. Persons with autism are often described by carers as seemingly lost in time.

In order to be able to organise our own lives better we make time concrete, visible in space with our watches and our calendars. This, of course, enables us to impose some sense of control over our lives. My argument is that persons with autism have the same basic needs as we do and therefore we have to develop what we may call 'autism-watches'. We need to give them concrete, visible, spatial answers to the very abstract question 'When?'

The answers need to be individualised at three different levels (Peeters and Gillberg 1999): the form of the symbol; the length; how the symbol is used.

The form

An ordinary child first understands words, then uses them expressively for communication. For a child who will eventually learn to communicate with objects, it is important also that he starts with the receptive side, that he learns that there is a meaning beyond the object. For example, each time when he goes to the free time area he is given a ball, when he goes to snack he is given a cup, when he goes to lunch he is given a plate, etc. This way he is being helped to make concrete associations between an object and an activity. It may, of course, be very threatening to parents who still hope their child will soon speak that a professional proposes the use of objects as the start of a communication program.

What can be useful in diminishing any threat is that parents have watched the assessment that has been made of their child. So they have seen that their child did not react to verbal instructions, did not imitate words, was not able to match pictures with objects, maybe did not even react to the sound items. All this seems to suggest that speech (the most abstract form of communication) will not be ideal for the immediate future.

In my own practice I tend to explain the advantage of using objects as a starting point by employing the image that in ordinary development speech is like an island that at once appears in an ocean of non-verbal communication. The biggest problem in autism is not speech but communication in general, also non-verbal forms of communication. In ordinary development children have developed so many functions of communication already before the first words appear (Watson *et al.* 1989; Layton and Watson 1995). Only a few days after giving birth mothers recognise: 'now she cries because she is hungry', 'now she cries differently because she needs attention' and so on. Before nine months the child looks at the mother/father and directs their attention towards something she finds interesting in the environment. In other words she is already making comments in a non-verbal way. Ordinary babies have had so many experiences that they understand well the power of communication when they discover an even more powerful form: speech.

It seems logical that children with severe communication problems learn to communicate in easy concrete ways, as with an object. It is important to know that forms are not necessarily permanent. A child learns to recognise the meaning of objects, and is then learning to see the relationship between objects and pictures before he uses pictures for receptive (and later expressive) communication. In the beginning the first objects may be very concrete and will be used in the next activity (e.g. the cup for snack, the plate for lunch). Later the objects may be of a more abstract nature (e.g. the cup will be checked in, but not used any more: on the snack table there will be another cup, the screw as a symbol for a work session for an adolescent with autism will not be used any more in the session itself, but checked in at the entrance of the work corner).

For some students the implication of important details in the objects is necessary, e.g. the use of objects of a certain texture for a student who still gets a lot of information from touching things. Other students will attach too much importance to colours and will not see that a red cup may have the same 'meaning' as a green cup. Due to this 'overselective thinking' it is important that the educational approach for such students is very well coordinated and that all carers use exactly the same symbols (in terms of size, colour, texture etc.) with students who still have not learned very well to generalise (Van Dalen 1995; De Clercq 1999; Verpoorten 1997).

Length

Usually persons concerned with offering predictability in time talk about timetables, day schedules, etc. Activities are then announced for a whole day or for half a day. Sometimes only three or two activities are announced, and often in the beginning only one (this may be all the student can understand in the near future – the sequence of two activities in a row may still be too difficult). Learning the meaning of objects may be seen as learning a new and very difficult language, so teachers need to recognise that pupils will be able to respond better if they do not start with too many 'words' at once. Building up a whole vocabulary of objects will be for later. Using the term 'vocabulary' also for objects is helpful for parents. It reminds me of a particular father. Each time I asked him how his son was doing, he answered sadly, 'He still does not speak.' And then months later when his son was in a classroom which specialised in autism, he said, 'He has a vocabulary of 50 photos.' So the term vocabulary should also be used when dealing with pictures or objects. But before the pupil can use his/her vocabulary expressively he/she has to understand its meaning first.

The use of the symbols

Some students with autism may be able to use a classroom agenda just like ordinary students. For students with autism and with the capacity to abstract meaning only at an object level, however, this is not an option. The first use of the symbol is probably when the teacher puts the object in the student's hands and guides him with the object to the corresponding place (e.g. ball to free time corner). This will probably need to be done several times before he is able to make the concrete association ball means free time. If the distance between the place where the symbol is given and the place of destination is too wide (and the student has a very young developmental age), it might be an advantage if the teacher first leads the student to the destination and shows him the object just before the activity (e.g. giving the plate not 20 metres before the entrance of the lunch area, but just before he sits down at the table and starts eating).

Later the distance between the moment the symbol is given and place/activity it stands for will grow. Afterwards new object-words will have to be added to his vocabulary but they all will be used in a similar way. In fact the teacher still continues to give the object to the student. Still later the student will make use of a real object-schedule. In a cupboard with different compartments each object from top to bottom will represent an activity or time-slot (e.g. cassette for music in the free time area, then box for work, the cassette again for free time, then glass for snack, then shoe for walking etc.). Until he sees and finds his bag at the bottom of the schedule. This bag means going home again. A very important step in the use of such an object-schedule is that the student himself becomes much more active and independent. If he is going to take the objects himself instead of being dependent upon the teacher's assistance, that also means that he is going to be able to situate himself in time in a more detailed and understanding way. He will not only understand what comes next but will also have some idea about the sequence of activities.

One could say that such a schedule really functions like an object-watch: the more objects that have been taken away from the schedule the fewer there are still to be seen. So the pupil directly sees time go by (perceptual synthesis versus conceptual analysis; time does not have to be analysed, it is perceived directly, the open analysis is replaced with information almost speaking for itself). Students who have reached this level of object-use very often also are able to handle a transition card that tells them to go and find the next symbol for the next activity (like saying in a non-verbal way, 'go and consult your agenda'). The transition card could be a card with the student's name or any card of a certain colour or form (sometimes the same for all students in one classroom).

A few teachers have told me about a difficulty they experience with a few exceptional students. These particular students seem to understand the duration concept when making use of an object-schedule, but seem to be too much fascinated by one or other (often favourite) activity on the schedule. Waiting for this activity to come seems impossible for them. Help in such a case always needs to be individualised, but often teachers then had to cover the later compartments of the object-schedule. Only the compartment for the next activity was left open. This way the student still had an idea of time to come without having the detailed information about the specific activities.

An augmentative educational approach: an illustration

I will now try to summarise some of the above issues by discussing a non-verbal child with autism and the parents' wish to develop his communication.

Bryan was a five-year-old non-verbal child with lots of behaviour problems. An evaluation showed that he had an overall two-year developmental level, with peak skills in eye–hand communication, but no emerging skills at all in the area of verbal communication. Also he was not able to see the relationship between a picture and an object. In fact Bryan was still at a 'pre-communication' level, he had not yet entered the symbolic world. His top performances in communication were that he put himself at the table when he wanted to eat something and at other times he pulled his mother or father by the arm towards the fridge. And there were lots and lots of problem behaviours: many of them being desperate attempts at communicating something for which he had no words or pictures or objects. His parents accepted that it would be a good idea to start with object-communication.

The very first beginning was at a receptive level. Bryan had to understand that there was a meaning beyond the objects, before he was going to be able to use objects to ask for things. In choosing the first 'word' ('object-word') it is important to start from the child's biggest motivation. When we asked Bryan's mother what he liked more than anything else in the world, the answer was 'spaghetti'.

His mother started the whole communication process in a very concrete way: with the fullest information possible. When she thought Bryan was hungry she went to him with a plate full of spaghetti (with the smell as extra-information so that there was no failure possible): 'Come'. And Bryan followed her with the plate in the kitchen. During subsequent days the information was made a little bit less concrete: less and less spaghetti, so that after a few weeks she only showed the plate and Bryan followed her into the kitchen. The receptive phase was a rather quick success.

But the transition from understanding to expressive communication may be much more difficult. From now on 'the service will be less perfect' and Bryan will need to experience that the initiative will have to come from him. When Bryan's mother thought he was hungry she would put the plate in front of him and ask with an open gesture: 'What do you want?' If he did not react she would point to the plate: 'What do you want?' She would push him close to the plate: 'What do you want?' and if he still did not take the initiative then his father would guide him physically and show him how to take the plate and give it to his mother. With the extra help of his father success was guaranteed. In the course of the following weeks the whole procedure was repeated and the levels of help decreased wherever possible from physical help, to pointing, to asking with an open gesture: 'What do you want?'

The teacher and teacher assistant also taught Bryan to communicate with objects as a first step and slowly the vocabulary of receptive and expressive communication increased. In the meanwhile Bryan's teachers were preparing all types of exercises at school to prepare him for another level of communication: with pictures. At school the teachers were also aware of the fact that Bryan needed a very concrete teaching style: even though he had a developmental age of two, verbal language as teaching approach may respond to our dream but not to reality. The verbal language had to be supported at an object level. Bryan, like all children with autism, needed an 'augmentative education'. Also, to make our expectations (e.g. teaching objectives in self-help skills, domestic skills etc.) more concrete we make use of objects. So we use object-communication at three different levels: (1) receptively (to make his life predictable); (2) expressively (to teach him to communicate his needs); (3) an augmentative teaching style.

I have explained this augmentative teaching style elsewhere (Peeters and Gillberg 1999). In this text I will only give one example. It is known that ordinary children in a certain developmental phase will speak aloud and that this language helps them to organise their play. Later on this 'external language' becomes 'internalised'. Inner language (a repertoire of concepts) helps us to get our behaviour organised. If someone asks me to 'clean the room' I understand the different detailed substeps included in this one word 'cleaning' (my 'inner language' or my 'brain script' helps me then to get my cleaning behaviour organised). Persons with autism, it seems, have less inner language than we often suppose and when we ask them to 'clean' the room, their inner language does not tell them how to carry out the different substeps involved. They may seem stubborn then, or lazy, but the real problem seems to be of a cognitive nature. It is not therefore a matter of 'bad boy' but rather of a lack of inner language. So written language, or pictures, or objects may serve as a compensation for the lack of inner language.

A certain person with autism may not 'know' what cleaning means, but when he 'sees' the pictures and follows them, then he gets his cleaning behaviour organised more easily. For persons who still have not reached the picture-level, object information may show them what to do: 'external communication' to compensate the lack of 'inner language'. So in the teaching of work skills, leisure skills, social skills, self-help skills and domestic skills the verbal teaching style is supported by more concrete information: pictures, objects.

In my view then an autism specific approach, an augmentative education, is the best possible treatment, based on the prevention of problem behaviour. It is important to understand that the problem behaviour is a symptom, just as the tip of the iceberg is the symptom of the iceberg (Schopler 1995). The most important part of the iceberg, however, is hidden under the water. The causes of the problem behaviours in autism are hidden, are invisible. It is important to understand these invisible causes and develop a treatment based on causes and therefore on prevention (Peeters and Jordan 1998). Persons who have autism in combination with a very young developmental age may have many 'problem behaviours' because we do not understand their way of thinking enough. In the following example of Charles you will see that objects communicate many things to him. If the carers around him do not understand the communication value of these objects, then they will react to the symptoms, not to the causes. Then the approach will be very disappointing, for them and of course for Charles. The key question is: is he 'a bad boy' or does he think differently?

At the end of one week practical training we always have a discussion on the 'problem behaviour' of the week (I will not go into details about the whole analysis). Charles was selected as he had been hitting himself very often during the week. Charles was an almost entirely non-verbal six-year-old child with autism with a very young developmental age. In fact the only word he said was 'mama'. He used it for every possible frustration or need. His fascination consisted of looking at cars. His parents admitted that they had a very difficult time at home. He would only sleep in a car, eat in a car and look at cars in his free time. His parents said that they simply had to give in often if they wanted to have a 'relaxed' time themselves, or have a night's sleep. We had started to teach Charles the use of symbols: a beaker was given before he had snack, a bib before he had lunch, a diaper before taking him to the toilet, a ball announced free time, a box to announce that he had activities to do at his desk, a bag became the symbol to return home. So Charles slowly learned to understand that there was a meaning beyond the perception.

There were problem behaviours at his desk. One time the participants had prepared a new task for him: taking balls from one box and putting them in another box. This was a terrible mistake since the ball had become the symbol for free time. When Charles saw the balls he wanted to go to free time. The participants made it clear he had to stay. Charles started hitting himself. Then he accepted and started doing the task. Unfortunately for Charles they had also forgotten to 'close' the second box, so that Charles continued to see the balls. Seeing these balls 'told' him: the task is not finished yet, I have to do everything all over again and he put them in the first box, then in the second and so on. He really did his best to understand what the participants had prepared for him. But the participants started talking to him: 'Charles, dat moet je niet doen. Als je de blokken in de doos gelegd heb, moet je ze laten liggen...' Not that they spoke Flemish. I put the comment in Flemish to give you an idea about the effect of speech on Charles. A combination of hearing the difficult speech with the balls he continued to see meant that he started hitting himself.

During our communication snack children have to ask for themselves in order to have the drinks and food in front of them. In such a 'sabotaged' situation, participants see how helpless some children are if they are not being helped all the time. In fact they may have words but not understand the real power (or the 'functions') of communication. Also our non-verbal Charles did not seem to understand yet that giving a plate to an adult to ask for eating might be more powerful than hitting himself. So during this snack Charles did not ask, even with his favourite biscuits in front of him. The conclusion of some of the participants was that he simply was not hungry; otherwise he would have asked for his favourite biscuits. Yet, when his group taught him how to ask for bread by giving a plate to an adult, he rather quickly understood the principle: 'I have to take the initiative and give something and in exchange I get something interesting back.' During that teaching session Charles went on asking with his plate till he had finished all of the bread!

So, it was not a question of not being hungry, but Charles still needed to discover the real power of communication with objects: when you're hungry you show a plate, it is that simple! Charles had discovered that day a very important step in the development of independence and self-esteem.

References

De Clercq, H. (1999) *Mama, Is Dit een Mens of een Beest? Over Autisme* (Mama, Is This an Animal or a Human Being? About Autism). Antwerpen: Houtekiet.
Gazzaniga, M. S. (1970) *The Bisected Brain*. New York: Appleton.
Happe, F. (1995) 'The role of age and verbal ability in the theory of mind task performance of subjects with autism', *Child Development* **66**, 843.
Jordan, R. R. (1996) 'Teaching communication to individuals within the autistic spectrum', *REACH. Journal of Special Needs Education in Ireland* **9**, 95.
Layton, T. and Watson, L. (1995) 'Enhancing communication in nonverbal children with autism', in Quill, K. (ed.) *Teaching Children with Autism*. New York: Delmar Publishing.

Peeters, T. (1997) *Autism: From Theoretical Understanding to Educational Intervention.* London: Whurr Publishers.

Peeters, T. and Gillberg, C. (1999) *Autism: Educational and Medical Aspects.* London: Whurr Publishers.

Peeters, T. and Jordan, R. R. (1998) 'The importance of training in the prevention of violence and abuse against people with autism', in Autism Europe (ed.) *Code of Good Practice on Prevention of Violence Against Persons with Autism.* Brussels: Autism Europe.

Schopler, E. (1995) *Parents' Survival Manual.* New York: Plenum Press.

Sinclair, J. (1992) 'Bridging the gaps: an inside-out approach of autism', in Schopler, E. and Mesibov, G. (eds) *High Functioning Individuals with Autism.* New York: Plenum Press.

Van Dalen, J. G. T. (1995) *Autisme: Weinig Keus?* (Autism: Not Too Much Choice). Engagement Special, NVA (Nederlandse Vereniging Autisme, Dutch parental society), P.O. Box 1367, Bussum, N 1400 BG, Netherlands

Verpoorten, R. (1997) *Kwalitatieve Stoornissen in de Waarneming* (Qualitative impairments in Perception). Antwerpen: In-service Opleidingscentrum Autisme.

Watson, L., Lord, C., Schaffer, B. and Schopler, E. (1989) *Teaching Spontaneous Communication to Autistic and Developmentally Handicapped Children.* Austin: Pro-Ed.

Chapter Three

Multisensory Education and Learners with Profound Autism

Flo Longhorn

This chapter examines the role of multisensory education in establishing a relationship leading to the potential for further education for Natalie – a very special person with profound autism, severe intellectual impairment and self-injurious behaviour.

Introduction

Natalie is a unique human being – a young woman with autism, profound intellectual disability and ceaseless self-injurious behaviour. She also has a hearty peal of laughter when she watches bubbles 'pop' or when a football rattle is rattled loudly near her ears. Natalie avoids human contact like the plague and is at her happiest in her own closed world of complex rituals and self-abuse. She feels very safe in her internal and external sensory world of selected sensations.

In order to provide any education or enable a learning process for Natalie, my objective had to be a simple one. I wanted Natalie to acknowledge me as a human being, relating to me in any manner she chose. Unless Natalie chose to do this, then her education would be a forced and meaningless interaction.

To do this, I needed to closely observe how Natalie interacted with herself and her immediate environment. Her world seemed to consist of sensations to do with ritualistic rocking and touch through self-physical abuse.

As I observed her, I could see patterns of routine. One of these was that she chose to sit on the floor, rock quickly with arms folded, hyperventilating and humming at the same time. I also observed that, when she got up to head bang, hit her face with her fist or smear faeces on her legs, she would play absorbedly with the results. Her senses were dominant in every respect of her rituals and routines.

Any friendly approach to Natalie was rebuffed vigorously with loud yells and overt physical threats. The only safe way into her world, to form a relationship,

appeared to be through the senses, especially those of:
- touch
- vibration
- vestibular sense
- pain
- physical energy.

I decided to make my first intervention through touch. Natalie seldom wears shoes and her feet are the furthest points from her body as she rocks on the floor. This would make my first contact less threatening.

Natalie's feet

As Natalie commenced her rocking ritual by spitting on the floor, sitting down with legs straight ahead, arms sternly folded, humming and hyperventilating, I took my shoes off. I sat down opposite her and placed my bare feet against her warm feet and started to follow her rhythm of motion. She carried on as if I did not exist. After half an hour (just as I was about to collapse with physical exhaustion), she stopped rocking, looked at our feet and then glanced at me. I acknowledged her glance and got up and left.

This was the first step in building a sensory relationship with Natalie. This has very slowly led Natalie to new sensory experiences, perceptual development, communication and a new relationship with the world around her.

Eighteen months later

The foot routine went on for months and, as the relationship built up, the glances and body language became stronger. One day, Natalie made it very clear to me that we had a relationship. She saw me come into the room, and then she angrily marched over to a cupboard. She took out a large pair of boots which she put on and commenced her rocking routine. She had vividly communicated to me that she held power in this relationship and her choice was *not* to relate today! She had very effectively blocked the sensory intervention. I took the hint and left.

Natalie has begun to initiate contact through bear hugs. As we sit on the floor, side by side now, she squeezes my waist until it hurts. When I squeeze back as hard as I can, she shrieks with delight. She also initiates fingernail-tapping play. She takes my hand and taps out an intricate tapping pattern on my fingers. She then gives me her hand and I do the same to her fingers, trying to repeat the sequence.

Natalie always makes sure I know the fragility of the relationship and the work I am doing. Recently, she took a musical box with a hinged mirror lid and smashed it on the floor, putting the shards of glass down her ears. A salutary lesson to take nothing for granted in my work.

Natalie's view of the 'feet' session*

'I was safely on the floor, building up a steady rhythm and feeling the effect of my heavy breathing. Suddenly, I felt a warm rocking contact on the soles of my feet. I did not want to stop my ritual and the feeling was a distance from my body, so I carried on. After a while, I could hear humming sounds, just like the ones I like to make, coming from the direction of the foot contact.

I had to take a quick glance at what was against my feet – and saw two other feet! Then I glanced at the person attached to them. The person acknowledged me briefly and then got up and left. I continued rocking until I was ready to start head banging.'

Natalie's viewpoint 18 months later*

'I think and act in very simple sensory or perceptual terms. My understanding of 'who I am' comes from the sensations of my body and the immediate environment. I am very aware of my internal and external body, which brings me great pleasure, although no one else sees it as pleasure. My actions form a very effective barrier to anything to do with relationships or the outside world. Not many people want to take me out into the world because I look awful and I behave so oddly. Not many people want to relate to me or to sustain the relationship because of how I behave most of the time. Suits me!

'I know that if I remain in my own carefully created world of sensations, very few demands can be made on me or my chosen lifestyle. My actions create anxiety, distress, disbelief and fear in other people. I have power because they think I might hurt them if I get a chance. I sense they feel failure because so many different regimes have been tried out on me – medication, restraints, confinement, protective clothing and behaviour programmes. They have all failed. I am still the same. I usually succeed in maintaining my sensory world order one way or another.

'I know I have a relationship with Flo, which started through our feet. I think the relationship is purely on my terms, as I still retain the power to terminate it

* *Note:* In examining Natalie's point of view of these experiences in the following sections, I act as her interpreter, as she chooses to use body, sound and behaviour for her means of total communication. She does not, as yet, use any formally recognised means of communication such as sign, symbol, objects of reference or spoken words (see Figure 3.1 for Natalie's first written communication). She has devised her own language.

Figure 3.1 Natalie's first written communication

whenever I want. She acknowledges this. The relationship is through my senses and not many scary demands are made on me. There appear to be no rules or regulations. Flo does not demand that I 'do things', but she takes things as they happen. There is little eye-contact, which pleases me. If I am in a really bad mood, Flo puts on an eye mask and her eyes disappear – this calms me down no end.

'The sensory sessions I have give me pleasure, as the sensations are the ones I like and crave most of all. I have also discovered that I have other senses, such as smell. Some of the materials are so interesting – a fierce vibrator which I can switch on and off, a humming toy bird to hold to my ear, rough sandpaper to scrape my skin, a smell of eucalyptus to make my nose hum. I stop for awhile and enjoy them instead of rocking or hitting.

'I've found that if Flo is very slow at getting materials to me, then I need to take her hand to exactly what I want and this encourages her to give it to me, more quickly. She seems to be even quicker if I point my finger.

'Flo is still learning my language. I think she understood it when I hit her on the chin, my favourite place to injure, and then I brushed it with a brush, just like she does to me. I like it. I wanted to share the sensation with her. She didn't look too happy though!

'I do now allow Flo to touch me. I like it when she wears gloves and touches me firmly. Sometimes I squeeze her tight around the waist and she squeezes me back tighter and we both shriek together.

'At the end of the day, I am still Natalie. I always go back to my rituals and routines, but I must admit that the sensory experiences on offer do tempt me to new sensory delights.'

The education perspective

The challenge of providing an education for Natalie is awesome. This is because her extreme behaviour and simple levels of intellect mask any potential to learn. She does not fit into any prescribed education, system of teaching or normal pattern of learning. Interestingly, her lifestyle is touched upon in the writings of people with autism. Jasmine Lee O'Neill (1999) writes,

> Autistics are captivated by movements and inner rhythms. They can become absorbed inside their own body rhythms, digestion, heartbeat, swallowing or breathing. Self stimulations aren't a behaviour problem. Those which seem self-injurious can be redirected into gentler actions. Body rocking whilst sitting is probably the stimmy that most people who know anything at all about autism are familiar with. Rocking connects with one's inner music. It is connected with a very deep primitive way of being soothed (p. 74).

Donna Williams (1996) talks about self abuse.

> The involuntary compulsion to self abuse is like a 'fit' or a sort of 'compulsion-vomit'. This purging sensation may well be either an attempt to sort of 'wash out' the system of

some form of information overload, or cause a shutting down of information accumulation (by abusing the body to trigger the perception of being under attack) in order to decrease the rate of incoming information (p. 304).

Both women give a deeper insight into Natalie's life style and a wider perception of her needs. Phoebe Caldwell (1998) also reflects on a way forward in describing her work with Mark.

> Mark, who has very special learning disabilities, self injures, hitting his head. He strokes his cheek with a circular movement when he is becoming upset. Mark shows interest when I echo his movement, first on myself and then on his cheek. When he is becoming disturbed, it is possible to distract him by drawing attention to a source of 'his' touch, which comes from outside himself (p. 28).

Phoebe takes the touch to another part of the body, away from the abuse. These observations from other people's insights create some optimism in planning for Natalie.

The first step is to go directly to the potential learner to ascertain her established self-taught activities. These may form a sensory framework upon which to build a more formal education. There is a need to:

- closely observe
- reflect upon what is portrayed
- plan action (with a great deal of lateral thought)
- continuously evaluate the educational situations.

Observations of Natalie over a period of time reveal three important factors for consideration in beginning an educational intervention. These are:

- her *multisensory world,* in which some senses have become distorted and some senses abandoned altogether;
- her *simple levels of intellect,* which reflect the early childhood patterns of thinking and concrete learning;
- the *prerequisites to learning,* which are lacking in her learning patterns.

Let us look at each area separately.

Natalie's multisensory world

We live in a multisensory world, in which a bombardment of sensory stimuli are transformed into sensations which give us information about:

- our internal body
- our external body
- our immediate environment
- the world beyond
- other human beings.

Even before we are born, our senses are alert and beginning to respond to the enclosed world around us. Our biggest sensory organ, the skin, is continuously massaged and caressed within the womb. As we develop physically, we are subjected to a range of bodily movement sensations including our own involuntary movements, rotation and our mother's movements. About three months before birth, ears begin to listen and react to sounds made both inside and outside the womb. Taste buds and five million smell receptors are awakening to prepare for the smell and taste of nourishment outside the womb.

At birth, we are ready to show a preference for smells and a liking for particular tastes, e.g. banana smells and milky tastes. As we are born, we tumble into a blinding world of visual confusion, although within eight weeks we are already differentiating between shapes, forms and colour with a preference for red, then blue. Soon we learn how to put two or three senses together for better effect – we snuggle into secure, warm arms, turning our heads to an interesting voice nearby and staring into a friendly face. We relate and bond to another human using a sensory platform which holds the five main senses – taste, smell, sound, vision and touch – but also holds many additional senses, such as weight, body position, balance and fatigue.

We are now aware that there are far more senses than the prominent ones of sound, vision, bodily experience, taste, touch and smell. The senses include all those shown in Figure 3.2. From this list, you can see why our senses can overwhelm us! A very special child may have the inability to process sensory information. He/she may make the decision to build on certain pleasurable senses to the exclusion of others. The sensory information that may get through to the brain has become fragmented, meaningless, unpredictable and often very scary. So the child sets up barriers, withdraws, has tantrums and then escapes into his/her carefully selected (and to them, safe) sensory world.

Hearing	Sight	Smell	Taste	Touch
Pressure	Heat	Cold	Pain	Weight
Gravity	Haptic touch	Cutaneous	Vibration	Rhythm
Thirst	Hunger	Fatigue	Nausea	Visceral
Motion	Lust	Sexuality	Sensuality	Numinous
Extrasensory perception		Conscious vision		Radiation sense
Physical energy		Balance (equilibrium)		Bending of joints
Position of the body (bodily experience)		Time track motion (past, present, future)		Vomeronasal sense (VNO)

Figure 3.2 Identifying the senses

In Natalie's case, she has, for her own reasons, selected the main senses of vibration, touch, sound, pain, vestibular and physical energy. She exists within these major senses to the exclusion of others and had made her environment safe but catastrophically limited for accessing the world beyond.

We have a major goal for Natalie in the multisensory world, which is: *Natalie will have the opportunity to access other senses and to broaden her access to the multisensory world.*

Natalie's simple level of intellectual development

Natalie is very much at a concrete level of thinking or perception and this hides much of the potential for perceptual development. Natalie does not present a clear picture to us, even when we view her through the multiple intelligence model of psychologist Howard Gardner (1985), comprising intelligence in:

- linguistics
- logic, mathematics, science
- visual and spatial awareness
- musical
- bodily, physical, kinaesthetic
- interpersonal
- intrapersonal awareness.

Natalie shows little perception in any of these areas of intelligence. The intellectual abilities that we can observe in Natalie fall firmly in the sensory concrete levels of simple perception. For example, Natalie knows about object permanence, as she can recognise herself in a mirror and she can manipulate objects with deft fingers.

When we consider Theory of the Mind (e.g. Baron-Cohen 1995), Natalie rarely shows an understanding of what others are thinking or experiencing. She really does not want to know what goes on in other people's minds. Her individual learning style is firmly placed in:

- her immediate environment
- her intimate social world of '1'
- her own emotions
- her bio-rhythms and bio-behavioural level
- her impulse-driven processing of information.

For Natalie, there must be one goal: *To enable her to access whatever level of intellectual development she can aspire to – but with dignity and respect to her status as a young woman.*

Natalie's prerequisites to learning

Natalie displays very few of the prerequisites to learning that are the tools for accessing learning, needed to progress in education and life. These prerequisites to learning (Longhorn 1993a) include:

- beginning to look and attend

- to communicate in any way
- to relate to self, to others, to the world beyond
- to play
- to coordinate the body
- to overcome behavioural barriers.

Without the development of these tools of learning, learners will have the following problems, clearly seen in Natalie's case. They will:

- seem to be unaware of themselves as a person
- put up behaviour barriers or stereotyped responses to exclude learning
- seem to be in a state of confusion as to what is happening in the world around them
- show a very slight or indifferent response to learning situations
- have an extremely short – or very selective – attention span
- appear unable to filter useful information from learning situations
- find it difficult to learn spontaneously
- show the odd isolated or obsessive skill
- be unable to link skills together
- have little sensory awareness or selective sensory awareness
- find it hard to interact with the world or people around them
- seem to have no fun and enjoyment in life as a whole.

Natalie's goal in this area has to focus on:

- *relationships*
- *communication*
- *overcoming behavioural barriers.*

The development of an individual sensory environment for Natalie

For Natalie, the first step in learning came through a 'foot' relationship. Once she had accepted the relationship, there was the opportunity to develop a very individual education programme for her. It was an opportunity to engineer the sensory environment in order to achieve the three main goals previously described. Natalie was to be offered sensory interaction leading to perceptual interaction and human interaction.

The reality of the educational environment for Natalie is that it needs a horizontal curriculum, to be presented in myriad different ways to the same learner. Natalie needs years in which to build up her skills and become spontaneous in her learning patterns. From the individual sensory environment came a set of new demands, the hidden curriculum. Structure was placed on each session through the medium of Natalie enjoying the session, having choice and preferences within it and being happy in what she was doing. The demands were for Natalie:

- to ask for a sensory experience by taking a hand to the activity, by pointing, by glancing at the activity and then at me;
- to know there is a beginning, middle and end to each session;

- to know the meaning of more, stop, '1,2,3', go!, used in the activities,
- to use cause and effect to extend sensory learning, for example by the use of a vibratory switch.

The sensory basket

The contents of Natalie's 'sensory basket' were crucial in enabling her to reach any of the hidden curriculum on offer. Let us look at each important sense for Natalie and how the materials were selected. The materials were changed or deliberately omitted regularly to make sure that obsessive use did not occur.

Sound

We perceive sound through the ears by vibrations transmitted by a wave movement of air particles from an object. Pure sounds can cause bodily changes. Biologists have discovered that different frequencies on the music scale can cause blood cells to change colour and shape. Certain sounds can also evoke body responses. For example, the sound 'mmmmmmm' which is a humming noise used by many autistic people causes the cranial nerves to vibrate and awakes energy.

Natalie's 'sound bank' included:
- greaseproof paper to blow on to vibrate
- loud football rattle
- electronic chirping hand-held bird, which vibrates when held
- metronome to rock to and fro
- balloons to vibrate noise on and to make rude noises
- alarm clock with a loud tick and alarm call like 'cock-a-doodle-doo!'
- toy trumpet
- long hollow tube through which you could 'mmmm' in her ear
- CD discs to tap on her teeth and spin.

The next step planned in her sound education linked closely to the use of vibratory music with treble bass on full strength. It also linked to one form of her communication, using her fingernail tapping, extended to tapping on my fingernails and tapping rhythms.

Touch

The sense of touch is the least specialised of the senses, but its sensitivity can be sharpened by use. Touch usually remains constant throughout our lives, unlike many of the other senses. Skin is the layered conveyor of touch and the sense is conveyed in the second level of skin. It is our 'all over' sensory organ that mediates temperature and pressure, excretes moisture, and feels pain and pleasure in different intensities throughout our body. The preferred texture for babies is rough and scratchy and this was certainly a preferred touch for Natalie. This preferred texture has been useful in beginning to offer Natalie an alternative to some self-injurious behaviour. Sometimes she will allow a strong bristle brush to be used on the opposite side of the head to that which she is hitting. She has started to brush her injured head with a brush – a tactile substitute for the feeling of pain.

Natalie's 'touch bank' included:

- metal pan scourers
- hand-held brushes of different shapes and with different bristles
- sandpaper of different grades of roughness
- combs
- stiff hair brushes
- fir cones
- metal pin circuit boards from an old computer
- loofah to scratch
- corrugated card to run the fingernails along.

The touch programme in later stages also included very simple leg massage. Natalie liked to smear faeces on her legs and also liked to smear the blood from the wounds she made when head banging. Natalie did not allow the use of ordinary massage oil on her skin, so an alternative had to be found. An aromatherapist made up a special aromatherapy cream containing oil of French lavender, frankincense and sandalwood. She made two pots, colouring one brown and the other bright red – for obvious reasons! Natalie liked the creams and busily rubbed them into her legs and also into the walls where she liked to head bang! Occasionally she let me rub the cream into her legs, affording the opportunity of using massage as a potential means of giving and receiving human communication – through touch.

As she is massaged, Natalie is exposed to a range of perceptual learning experiences:

- a feeling of bodily awareness
- enhanced sense of touch
- a sensory communication
- alleviation of stress and tension through the aromatherapy oils
- slowing of mood and temper
- concentration on real enjoyment.

If Natalie refused the creams, the oils were added to water and sprayed into the air around her.

Vibration

Vibration can be offered through mechanical means as opposed to self-inflicted vibration through head banging and head hitting. This forms the most basic of sensory levels of interaction with oneself or with an object. Temple Grandin (1995), an adult with autism who works as an animal behaviourist, devised a 'squeeze body' machine to use on herself to become familiar with being hugged. The machine incorporated vibration so she could relax and enjoy the pressure.

The vibration initially used with Natalie was linear vibration with a few fixed frequencies, ranging from a tickle to robust vibration, which gave a percussion effect to the body. Although it is advised that vibration should not be applied to the head, this was Natalie's favourite place!

The sensory basket contained a selection of vibratory equipment, including:

- battery operated vacuum cleaner
- vibratory cushions
- hand-held vibrators
- vibratory eggs
- massage vibrating tube
- vibratory wobble ball
- CD disks to tap and vibrate on the teeth
- electronic toothbrush
- vibrating pig with massaging nose.

Natalie soon learned to switch things 'on' and 'off' and increase the vibration patterns. From the vibration sessions there is a range of future goals to enhance Natalie's perceptual learning. The future programme includes:

- a vibratory foot bath
- a vibrating switch that is connected to a bubble tube – pressing the switch activates a glowing, noisy tube, to show cause and effect
- use of vibratory music to explore the range of sounds not accessed by Natalie, such as drum music.

Implications for pedagogy

- Education begins with the focus on the learner and not a set of prescribed education handed down from on high.
- The senses breach the barrier into the world of special people and form a platform from which to go forward together in their education.
- A toolbox of skills needs to be offered to the very special learner so he/she can access learning more easily.
- It takes years to get anywhere!

In conclusion

Natalie has slowly entered the field of education and begun to use her senses and perceptions in a more normal way. She still spends the majority of her time in her rituals and obsessions. However, she is now open to new experiences and her communication is slowly expanding. What is the future for Natalie? The life experiences for Natalie will remain very restricted and constrained. Her potential for leading a fuller life is dependent on a realisation by those who surround her each day that she is a unique human being and not an embarrassing enigma to be hidden from view.

References

Baron-Cohen, S. (1995) *Mindblindness: An Essay on Autism and Theory of Mind.* Cambridge, MA: M/T Press.

Caldwell, P. (1998) *Person to Person – Establishing Contact and Communication with Profound Learning Disabilities and Extra Special Needs.* Brighton (UK): Pavilion Publishing.

Gardner, H. (1985) *Frames of Mind: The Theory of Multiple Intelligences.* London: Granada Publishing.

Grandin, T. (1995) *Thinking in Pictures.* New York: Doubleday.

Longhorn, F. (1988) *A Sensory Curriculum for Very Special People.* London: Souvenir Press.

Longhorn, F. (1993a) *Prerequisites to Learning for Very Special People.* Bedford (UK): Catalyst Education Resources.

Longhorn, F. (1993b) *Planning a Multisensory Massage Programme for Very Special People.* Bedford (UK): Catalyst Education Resources.

O'Neill, J. L. (1999) *Through the Eyes of Aliens.* London: Jessica Kingsley.

Williams, D. (1996) *Autism – an Inside-out Approach.* London: Jessica Kingsley.

Chapter Four

Intensive Interaction and Children with Autism

Melanie Nind

Introduction

Kris and Lindsey

Kris, a young adult with autism, is roaming around the classroom, repeating sounds to himself. Lindsey, his teacher approaches, face on, and places her hands on his shoulders, squeezing playfully and saying in a playful, rhythmic, almost daring tone, 'Are you going to play with me? Are you? Go on, go on!' Kris turns his head to the side and continues with his vocalising. The sounds indicate that his mind is elsewhere, the impact is blocking. Lindsey places her hand over his mouth, on and off, on and off, immediately changing the nature of the sound. This initiates a known game in their repertoire. Kris narrows his eyes in a frown of concentration, dips his head forward slightly and becomes interested. There is a visible switch of mood as a half-smile appears. After a few seconds Kris becomes silent.

Lindsey continues the hand over mouth action and imitates the sound. Kris is still and silent and she changes the game to another in their repertoire. She presses his nose, again playfully daring in her simple, repetitive speech, 'go on, go on' and she regains his half-smile and attentive expression. Seconds later Kris is on the move again, this time with Lindsey accompanying him. She keeps up the intermittent nose-game and her verbal commentary, 'What are you doing? What are you doing? You, you!' Her voice is playful and light; there is a rhythmic, repetitive pattern to the words.

Kris pauses in his wandering and simultaneously Lindsey changes her action to a slower, more gentle drawing her finger down the length of his nose in rhythmic pairs of little strokes accompanied by 'Gotcha, gotcha!' Kris furrows his brow and attends to her actions, vocalising with a sound she treats as an indication of his interest; his face is poised in a half-smile. She then builds her actions and words bigger and bolder and he turns his posture and face slightly towards her. He dips his head down to her, giving it an excited shake. His attention is fully on the game now and his smile is full and warm. Lindsey introduces pregnant pauses before turns of pressing his nose, she uses careful timing and each time whispers 'ready', building his anticipation and holding his attention. This part of the game lasts for ten bursts of activity, during which Kris offers fleeting, easy-to-miss glimpses of eye-contact.

The game continues with phases of wandering and intermittent playful exchanges, Lindsey commentating on their joint actions, placing her hand over his mouth during his vocalising and giving him sideways cheery hugs. At one point Kris allows himself to be guided into a corner where he can be completely still; he relaxes, leaning against the wall and enjoys a burst of the nose-pressing game. On this occasion Kris enters into the turn-taking, putting his head forward each time to trigger the turns of his teacher; he becomes fully engaged, smiling and daring to look. There is tension in the playful atmosphere and then he pushes forward. They enjoy some more turns on the move, this time less intense, until his mood changes, his movements become quicker, his expression becomes more distant and Lindsey does not attempt to resume the game.

Billy and Kerry

Billy, who is three, is in the sensory room, excitedly flapping and looking round. He makes a high-pitched vocalisation and Kerry, his teacher, repeats the sound back to him. He notices her, approaches to where she is kneeling and climbs on her back for a familiar rough and tumble game. She dramatically gradually tips him forward, and then with a sudden 'hup' raises him up again. Billy laughs, looks round distractedly, and then squeals and jumps on her back for more. Kerry repeats the game, more slowly this time, counting her way down '... one ... two ...'. He climbs off and she leans back on her heels so she can look up into his face; they exchange a brief look.

Billy circles the room, squealing and flapping excitedly at the lights. Kerry stays where she is and when Billy gets near she widens her eyes and takes an exaggerated breath, signalling she is ready to play. They repeat the game, he wanders again, and then they repeat it once more. This time Kerry tips him further so he rolls right over the top; she asks in a high-pitched, questioning tone 'Again? Again?' Next time she tips him to the side as she exclaims 'Down!' He then becomes distracted again, flapping and exploring the room. She tries to draw him back into the game by playfully leading in with 'one ..., two ..., three ...'. She doesn't succeed this time so she changes the lighting in the room and follows his gaze upward. He moves behind the blinds and she attempts to make this into 'peek-a-boo'. He isn't interested in this but he moves around for more of the rough and tumble. When his interest next fades she joins in with the tempo, tone and volume of his vocalising while rhythmically shaking him in playful bursts.

After more roaming and then more rough and tumble Billy begins to wander off, but Kerry holds on to his hand and he flops down in front of her. She puts her legs over his (as if to play 'row the boat') and walks her fingers up his chest to tickle him under the chin. They both laugh and, holding Billy's attention, Kerry begins a slower, gentler version of the tickle routine, followed by a one-fingered version. Then with her whole hand she counts her way up his chest culminating in pulling him up for a playful hug. In the next turn of the game Kerry leaves a longer, more pregnant pause and they laugh and squeal loudly together when the tickle finally comes. The tempo changes again and, with his attention on her, Kerry slowly and dramatically moves her hand down from her face on to his face. He gazes up at her, his attention on her complete, and moves his hand like hers as if to ask for more. In the turns that follow Kerry introduces more variations to the game by blowing on his hands, and imitating his hands covering his face. This moves seamlessly into a game of 'peek-a-boo' – each peeping out between their fingers, with Billy flapping gently in anticipation and the pair laughing together.

There follows more tickling and Billy wriggles away ready to climb on Kerry's back again; she modifies the routine by laying down and looking up a him, he steers the game back round to rough and tumble, and she tips him forward again so they are face-to-face. He lies looking up at her, and relaxed he explores her face, tracing her features with his fingers, and then feeling his own face. They are both silent and absorbed. He rolls away and they have a few more turns of familiar routines, before he wanders off again, this time to the door and out.

Analysis of the sessions

Each of the vignettes in this chapter describes a session of Intensive Interaction between an individual with autism and learning difficulties and his teacher. They are both taken from video of real sessions. I will comment on each session as I imagine it seems to the person with autism, although there are acknowledged huge assumptions in this. Then, in analysing the sessions from the teachers' perspective, I will draw out the principles of the interaction that are common to both and that underpin the teaching approach.

Child's perspective – Kris

In the first vignette the young person with autism is generally more distant and less motivated by the social world than the child described later. He is a restless person, who is roaming before settling into the repetitive, ritualised activity that largely fills his days. For him this will be filling a particular beaker with water and pouring it out of a particular window on to a particular spot below. His teacher intrudes upon his isolation, but because he has not yet become absorbed in his water pouring he does not seem to mind too much. Also he does not object or resist because she is very familiar to him and everything she does is also quite familiar. This means that although she moves into his personal space he is not alarmed or unduly stressed. They have established a few simple, playful interactive routines in their repertoire which means that Kris has learnt that Lindsey is not too unpredictable and that she has the potential to offer something of interest.

Lindsey's intrusion into Kris's world does not make big demands on him. He does not have to comply with her agenda or try to make sense of situations that are too complex for him to understand. She alters his self-stimulation. The sounds he makes and hears in his head are changed and this catches his attention. He is not sure what to do with this and he stops making the sounds. He hears her making sounds like his and this interests and pleases him. She is doing the things he likes doing.

She is intruding upon him in short bursts; short enough for him to be able to enjoy them without becoming overwhelmed. If he feels at all edgy he can move around, which he finds calming. This means he feels in control of the situation. The person near him is not going away but she is not overruling or demanding too much of him either. He has the urge to roam the room, but he is interested too and this means he is pulled in two directions. He allows himself to be backed into the corner where he can be still. This allows him to focus just on the teacher and the activity and to enjoy it. The timing of what happens is rhythmically structured and this helps him to anticipate when it is next to happen. The activity itself centres on him, making it familiar and motivating, and he begins to relax. When he needs things to become less intense he can make them so by moving around again. This helps him be more confident with the activity and he gets more involved next time, making things happen by taking his turn – with dips of his head he maintains the exchange.

What follows is not unexpected and he enjoys the feeling of leading this person in their interactive dance. This is all still quite new and challenging though, so after going so far as to look at the teacher he needs to disengage and retreat into isolation once more. Knowing that he can do this – that the ending of the activity is under his control – means that he will be willing to interact again. Knowing that he can lead what happens and that he can experiment with tiny changes in a safe environment means that he might do something a bit different next time. Knowing that interacting with the other person felt good to him means that he is getting to like spending time with her and that the foundations of a relationship are gradually developing.

Adult's perspective – Lindsey

The teacher in this interaction is not aimless. She wants to attract and hold the attention of the learner and she wants them to share something together. She wants this to be as reciprocal and enjoyable as she can enable it to be. For this to happen she knows that the interaction has to be on Kris's terms – paced and led by him. Even though she has to do most of the work to get the interaction started and keep it going, she is reliant on his signals to guide her. Moreover she is reliant on her ability to interpret very idiosyncratic feedback and to operate in the absence of encouragement if necessary.

She has used Intensive Interaction with other learners and is confident with the principles she is using and her own ability to enact them meaningfully. She knows how to initiate an interaction and then become follower rather than leader by being contingently responsive (responding contingently involves responding, closely in time, to something the other person does; this may be by imitating a behaviour, celebrating it or commenting on it; it may be by changing one's pace or activity, but it must be triggered by the communication partner). She has chosen her time to begin carefully, based on her knowledge of Kris and when he is likely to be receptive. She has a small repertoire of familiar games that she has built up with Kris and she knows that these provide them with a safe starting place. She also knows that she has to be open to opportunities to vary the games and to recognise and celebrate any variations that he makes. She enjoys interacting with him in this way and this helps to keep her relaxed and playful. She gives a natural running commentary of their activity and this helps to set the atmosphere and pace. She knows when to push on and when to hold back, partly based on intuition and partly on experience and reflection on previous interactions. She is skilful in her use of timing, voice, face and body language, but much of this is at a subconscious level. Later she will think about what was effective and why, but while she is interacting her judgements are swift as she continually adapts her actions to maintain optimum levels of involvement.

Child's perspective – Billy

Billy is less self-absorbed than Kris though he still finds greater attraction in objects and their properties than in other people. He is often seemingly at the mercy of his senses, being drawn to things or scared away by the way they look or feel or sound. The lights in the sensory room excite him but other distractions are minimal. The teacher in the room does not interest him unless he can use her as a plaything. His attention is caught by her sounds, which are like his sounds, and he remembers the enjoyable sensation of rough and tumble games with her. He is happy to be jiggled and swayed and thrown about; this is undemanding and pleasing to his senses. Sometimes he is 'caught unawares' by something new or different in the rough and tumble play. He has to process this, sometimes taking time out of the contact to do this. By moving in and out of the interaction he is learning to self-regulate. He is also learning that Kerry has enormous potential as a plaything. (With more time spent with her, his enjoyment of her on a more personal level may also develop.)

Billy goes through many bursts of familiar activity interspersed with small variations and new developments in the routine. His enjoyment and his ability to largely pace and control the activity helps him to relax and to be able to attend to Kerry. He becomes interested enough in her to want to explore how she looks and feels and how she will respond. He is learning that he can achieve a response from her – he can make things happen. He is practising new skills – over and over, the way children do – and he is enjoying doing this with a supportive other person. He is trying new things and retreating to the familiar whenever he needs to.

Adult's perspective – Kerry

Kerry is relatively new to special education and to autism, but she is comfortable with children and children's play. She is happy to be on the floor romping with Billy. Her primary goal is to build a relationship with her pupil so that their time together can be meaningful and enjoyable. She has learnt the kinds of physical play he enjoys and she is content to join in with this – to let him rehearse the limited communication abilities he has within this safe yet fun framework. She is also aware of the potential within it to help move Billy on. She is thinking all the time about possible variations in their play. She is consciously using extension opportunities to hold attention for a few seconds longer or to get one more glimpse of eye-contact. At the same time she is having her own fun, genuinely enjoying the game. She is also taking the time to learn more about what motivates Billy, how much interaction of what kind he can cope with before becoming overloaded, and how she can use her own interpersonal skills to engage with him. After the session she records what happened, what the highlights were and how the session felt for her. On this particular occasion she is particularly pleased with the two quiet interludes as this gentle exploration is new for them.

Explanatory account of the episodes

Both teachers described above are using Intensive Interaction (Nind and Hewett 1994). Their interactive play is different in many ways, influenced by their personalities, preferences, intuitions, and the experiences of their interactive partners. What they have in common, however, is interaction based on a set of principles derived from a developmental perspective and analysis of normal caregiver–infant interaction. These principles are as follows.

- Interactions should be mutually enjoyable; the primary purpose is to enjoy each other and the primary focus is the quality of the interactive process.
- The teacher should adjust her interpersonal behaviours (gaze, voice, linguistic style, body posture, facial expression) to become attractive and meaningful to the interactive partner.
- The pace of the interaction should depend on the interactive partner; it should not be rushed; there will be pauses, repetitions, blended rhythms, peaks and troughs in activity levels.
- The teacher should impute intentionality in the behaviour of the interactive partner, that is, credit the learner with thoughts, feelings and intentions and respond to behaviours as if they have communicative significance, thus drawing the person into a pseudo-dialogue.
- The teacher's actions should be contingent on the actions of the interactive partner, following the learner's lead; she should continuously observe and interpret non-verbal feedback and make micro-adjustments based on this feedback, to achieve optimum levels of attention and arousal.

In Intensive Interaction these principles guide the teacher who tries to facilitate frequent short bursts of quality interaction and to incorporate this style of interaction in her everyday processes. Many of these principles will be followed without conscious thought through allowing oneself to be relaxed and playful and by responding intuitively. This will be combined at times with much more conscious employment of the principles based on careful reflection on what is needed and yet is not coming easily. Usually narrative and video records are kept to inform a team of practitioners, in a positive problem-solving framework, about how best to support the development of interactions that are conducive to social, communication, cognitive and emotional development.

The rationale for the approach is that all learners (and especially those with complex learning disabilities) need sound foundations for learning in the form of good early experiences and the development of fundamental communication and social abilities (whatever their age). Without these they may be taught skills (such as being still when someone is talking), or they may acquire all sorts of other abilities, some of them apparently more sophisticated (such as giving the Makaton sign for drink), but they may not understand the essence of what it is to communicate and to be social. It is this central understanding of fundamental concepts such as: 'I am good to be with, other people are good to be with, we can share meaning, I can elicit responses in others, I can communicate intentions' etc., with which Intensive Interaction is concerned. This kind of learning is almost impossible to break-down into small steps and *teach*, but it is *learnt* almost without notice in normal development, through the processes of interaction between infants and their caregivers (Brazelton *et al.* 1974; Schaffer 1977).

Intensive Interaction attempts to use the intuitive pedagogy of the child-led, nurturing interactive style of parents, in very different circumstances with learners of all ages who are at the earliest stages of communication and social development. Differences in the interactions are necessitated by this being education rather than parenting and because here the development of a relationship is just a part of wider learning aims. Differences also emerge from the disabilities of the learners. The behaviour of individuals with autism – the way they are – inevitably has an impact on what happens in the interaction between them and others. Irascibility, preoccupation, hyper-sensitivity to sensory stimuli, lack of feedback, or absence of mutual gaze, all make the natural flow of interaction difficult to get going or sustain. In these circumstances the teachers' intuitions may not suffice and choice of interactive style needs to become more explicit, and used with deliberate purpose and greater intensity and reflection. Teachers need to learn to use a version of the facilitative style of nurturing without it being triggered by the child, and to sustain it in the face of adversity, while still retaining a sense of the child leading the interaction. They need to learn about good times to approach and good things to try, and what to do if an individual pushes away or another doesn't respond at all.

Intensive Interaction and its basis in the normal developmental model are described in more detail in *Access to Communication* (Nind and Hewett 1994). There are published accounts of parents and teachers using this approach with children with autism (Hewett and Nind 1998), and discussions of the evidence of its usefulness and theoretical relevance for children with autism are also documented (Nind 1999; Nind and Powell in press). In the next section I try simply to draw out the teaching and learning issues involved with Intensive Interaction and autism and illustrate why a pedagogy that is not special to autism has relevance for children with autism.

Implications for pedagogy

The opening chapter of this book highlights some of the ways in which the nature of learning in autism is distinctive and the challenges to teaching that follow from this. When we consider how difficult the social world is for someone with autism we must surely marvel at how easily non-autistic, normally developing children learn from their interactive experiences. One could argue that this is because of the (social) learning template that the child brings or because of the optimum interactive style that the caregiver employs. However, the more complex reality is that successful learning arises from the interaction that occurs *between* the two partners – what is important is the good 'fit' or 'match' between what each needs and provides (Warren and Rogers-Warren 1984). This good fit applies to the content of the interactions being developmentally right for the child's level, the pace being right, the activity being sufficiently motivating, and so on. Whatever one thinks about the learning style of the child with autism, the concept of a teaching approach that allows for a good fit is equally relevant. This raises the issue of whether one can define a teaching method that fits well with all children with autism, or one that fits well with all children regardless of autism, or whether a guiding principle like contingent responsiveness allows for a good fit with each individual and their idiosyncrasies. It also raises the question of whether a good fit for a child with autism is necessarily an 'autistic' interactive style.

A transactional or interactionist perspective allows us to focus on what goes on *between* teacher and learner (although in reality, both are learners, learning about how to be effective with the other). Traditionally deficit models have focused on the child's problems and putting these right. In autism there is also some history of parent blaming and correcting parental deficits. Looking instead at the transactions and interactions appropriately focuses teaching efforts on what happens between the communication partners as part of a fluid, complex process. A pedagogy for autism needs to address the quality of this process and the interactive match.

Intensive Interaction takes this interactive perspective and uses a naturalistic approach based on a normal developmental model. This does not mean one has to ignore the difficulties of the child with autism (nor over-simplify them), but it allows for placing those difficulties in a complex social context. Part of this context is the social world of the teacher that allows for supporting her in examining and adjusting her part of the interactive exchange to improve the fit and enhance the feelings of effectiveness for both parties.

Does a good fit mean an autistic style for the teacher? The argument is frequently made that children with autism do not, or can not, learn through social means. This may lead us into contriving all sorts of other ways of teaching other things, and there are even attempts at teaching and learning about the social world *asocially*. The alternative response to difficulty with social learning is to learn about the social world and about learning socially *through* social interaction. This may be facilitated by a particular kind of social interaction that is very supportive and fine-tuned to match the child's needs. This stance is taken in Intensive Interaction and is best illustrated with some examples.

Theo Peeters and Stuart Powell, in this volume, discuss the autistic difficulty with meaning. A child with autism may not be searching for social meaning, but in Intensive Interaction that potential for social meaning is made very accessible and explicit in the interactive play. In particular, the way in which the teacher treats the child's behaviours as social almost spells out meaning (such as when you tip your head forward this means you want another turn). In addition, children may have their own idiosyncratic meanings and a great deal of difficulty in gaining access to shared meaning. In Intensive Interaction the teacher facilitates the process of the idiosyncratic becoming shared by assuming the responsibility of doing most of the adjusting. That is, the child is not expected to make the huge step of learning the adult's meaning, but rather the emphasis is on the teacher sharing the child's perspective and joining in at their level, establishing the shared connections on territory that is safe and meaningful for the child (and moving on together from there). The teacher may never be sure that she knows what the child is thinking, but this need not be a block to communication and shared meaning. All communication is about *negotiating* meaning and not about pure messages sent and received untainted. The process of ascribing and interpreting meaning may not be perfect, and shared meaning or the search for social meaning may not develop to the full extent, but we do not need to avoid this territory altogether.

There are other examples that can illustrate Intensive Interaction with children with autism. In ordinary or even ideal situations of child development the adult clearly has a role in enabling the child to be part of a reciprocal exchange. In Intensive Interaction this enabling role is likely to be extended, both in quality and in duration. The familiar, ritualised games that typify early interactions provide a structure for each interactive partner to play a part and a safe environment for the child to explore, experiment and begin to predict. In Intensive Interaction with a child with autism, the repertoire of games might be more limited or more basic and the rituals might be more idiosyncratic to the child's preferences, but the game-playing still performs the same function. The world is brought within the child's control and made meaningful and predictable.

The child with autism may have difficulties with relating his/her own experiences to the experiences of others, but in Intensive Interaction the experiences of the interactive partners are interwoven, and again this happens at a very basic and meaningful level and in a very safe context. It is suggested that the child with autism may experience events at an objective/perceptive level rather than subjectively. Again one can try to work round this, or one can try to facilitate the beginnings of subjective experiencing (and of intersubjectivity). For the latter approach there is a need for emotional as well as intellectual arousal. In Intensive

Interaction the achievement of pleasure and *mutual* pleasure is central; teachers seek to enable the child to enjoy the learning, and to be aware that this enjoyment is shared. Furthermore, here teachers seek to intellectually and emotionally arouse the child and to enable the child to learn to self-regulate this arousal.

This self-regulation, of course, connects with another area of difficulty in autism, a sense of agency – the understanding that one can cause an effect on the world, or on oneself, and that others can do this too. In the natural model adults support the development of this sense of agency through many aspects of their interactive play. Responding contingently to the child and imputing intentionality are particularly important for this. Responsiveness sets the child up so he/she cannot help but make things happen and the use of timing and drama in the interaction makes this agency explicit. Responding by imitating can be especially salient for the child. Responding as if intention was there highlights that intention is possible and what can be achieved. This may be problematic in autism, but the natural pedagogy is powerful and can be made even more powerful by augmenting it with layers of reflection.

In Intensive Interaction then, the response to a child with an autistic style of interacting and thinking is not an autistic style of interaction; it is not to simplify the social experience so that interactions become rule-bound and stilted. Rather the response is to be even more creative in our interactions. We are not matching a learning style that lacks subjective meaning and connectedness with experiences that are devoid of these aspects, but rather with experiences in which these are rich, intense and accessible. The template of normal development is not suspended, but we do not allow assumptions based on it to prevent us from interacting in different ways and perhaps without the feedback and responses that usually feed the positive cycle of interaction. Instead we value the idiosyncratic behaviour and perspective of children with autism, working on their terms, negotiating a world in which we can make connections and be social and communicative with each other in some way.

Through exploring how young infants learn, and devising from this principles for enabling children with severe and complex learning disabilities to learn, we have suggested that some principles are key and that these are much more widely generalisable. These are that:
• the learner should be active;
• the learning should be instrinsically motivating;
• the learner should share some control of the learning activity.
One can always find exceptions to deny such principles any universal status. Indeed social constructionist psychology highlights that in some senses these are culturally specific. One way of understanding children with autism is to see them as outside of the culture with a different perspective altogether. Are we wrong then to impose such principles on children with autism? Is this some kind of cultural imperialism? I would suggest that this is not the case, and that the principles still apply, as long as we are not imposing our version of what is motivating. Intensive Interaction does not insist that social is the best or only way, but seeks to open up possibilities of children *learning how to learn through social interaction*.

Intensive Interaction, then, can be regarded as more of a remedial than compensatory approach. It takes into account the effects of autism, but also directly addresses the autism itself in a therapeutic sense. In Intensive Interaction we work on establishing the foundations for learning in the social and communication domains. Learning here may always be flawed, different or difficult, but attempting to teach without these foundations, with the child and adult on separate islands and with no attempt to build bridges between them, does not seem a viable alternative. Making the best possible bridge does not mean that both parties have to put in the same amount of work in the same way, but it does require a basic plan and good support structures. It also involves both parties learning about bridge building. It involves children with autism learning how to learn.

To sum up, the key teaching and learning principles from the interactionist perspective of Intensive Interaction are as follows. The quality of the interactions between children and adults are enhanced by the adults using elements of the caregiver–infant nurturing style such as adjusted interpersonal behaviours, relaxed tempo with pauses, rhythm and repetition, imputing intentionality, responding contingently and creating mutually enjoyable interaction routines. In this way there is a good fit between what the child likes and needs in interaction and what the adult offers. Social interaction becomes intrinsically motivating and meaningful and the child learns how to learn socially. In combining intuitive responding with careful reflection teachers are able to augment natural processes rather than replace them with more contrived learning situations.

References

Brazelton, T. B., Koslowski, B. and Main, M. (1974) 'The origins of reciprocity: the early mother–infant interaction', in Lewis, M. and Rosenblum, L. A. (eds) *The Effect of the Infant on its Caregiver*. New York: Wiley.

Hewett, D. and Nind, M. (eds) (1998) *Interaction in Action: Reflections on the Use of Intensive Interaction*. London: David Fulton.

Nind, M. (1999) 'Intensive Interaction and autism: a useful approach?', *British Journal of Special Education* **26**(2), 96–102.

Nind, M. and Hewett, D. (1994) *Access to Communication: Developing the Basics of Communication with People with Severe Learning Difficulties through Intensive Interaction*. London: David Fulton.

Nind, M. and Powell, S. (in press) 'Intensive interaction and autism: some theoretical concerns', *Children & Society*.

Schaffer, H. R. (ed.) (1977) *Studies in Mother–Infant Interaction*. London: Academic Press.

Warren, S. F. and Rogers-Warren, A. (1984) 'The social basis of language and communication in severely handicapped preschoolers', *Topics in Early Childhood Special Education* **4**, 57–72.

Chapter Five

Musical Interaction and Children with Autism

Wendy Prevezer

Introduction

Tina, a four-year-old girl who has been diagnosed as having severe autism, is in the music room with Ginny, her teacher. Tina does not yet use any spoken language. There is also a 'music specialist' at the keyboard, facing into the room with a clear view. Throughout this session, the two adults work closely together. Whilst Ginny plays directly with Tina, Wendy accompanies and supports the interaction, responding with her voice and keyboard, with detailed attention to the timing, mood and energy of their movements and sounds. Four distinct episodes within the session are described below.

A 'flexible' action song

Tina is sitting back on a soft low chair, with Ginny on the floor in front of her, so that their eyes are more or less level. Ginny taps Tina's feet together rhythmically as she sings, 'Tap your feet, tap your feet, tap your feet like this …'. Sometimes she pauses within the song, momentarily halting the flow. Tina sometimes makes eye contact in these pauses, or pushes her feet back in to Ginny's hands, and the song then continues immediately. At one point, Tina pulls her feet out of Ginny's hands and briefly taps them together herself: Ginny immediately leans back, raises her own feet, and joins in with Tina so that they are tapping in synchrony.

Meanwhile with each repetition, Ginny gradually pulls Tina closer in a playful way, until she is on her lap on the floor, and they are holding hands. In subsequent verses of the song Ginny offers different actions, such as 'Bouncy bounce' or 'Twist around', watching Tina's face and body language closely for feedback and emotional responses. Some of these verses are simply ideas offered by Ginny or Wendy: others are based on a small movement that Tina does spontaneously. When she leans back, Ginny sings the words 'Row your boat' to the same song, helping her to cooperate in the traditional pulling action, although her back is stiff and it is hard to get a flow of movement.

A 'set' action song

They switch to the familiar tune, 'Row, row, row your boat', repeating it several times. Within it they develop exaggerated wobbling movements and sustained vocal sounds on the word 'merrily'. Whenever Tina wobbles her hands or body, the words and tune of 'merrily merrily' are repeated. This part of the song is repeated as many times as Tina wobbles, with an atmosphere of some intensity and excitement as she begins to do it intentionally. Eventually the song is concluded in its traditional way with straight rocking.

A pre-verbal 'conversation'

Ginny stands aside, giving Tina some space. Tina approaches the video camera, looks at her reflection in the lens, and makes some vocal sounds. These are tuneful and controlled, and include her own characteristic vocalisation, 'odio-dio-dio-dio-dio'. Ginny repeats these sounds gently back to her, supported by Wendy's keyboard and voice. Tina vocalises more, listening for a response each time, sometimes varying the pitch and syllables slightly. They take turns a few times, and occasionally sing the same sounds in synchrony. Tina acknowledges Ginny's participation with eye-contact and smiles. She suddenly makes a quiet snorting sound after 'odio-dio', and this is soon incorporated, with gentle humour, into the conversation. For a few moments there is a real two-way flow, as either partner can initiate the sequence of sounds, and the other anticipates and adds the snort.

A physical play routine

Tina climbs onto a small chair and looks back over her shoulder. Ginny approaches with her arms outstretched, asking 'Jump?' and watching for feedback. Tina does not indicate clearly what she wants, but seems to be waiting to be lifted. With a long exaggerated 'And…', Ginny lifts her down, saying '…jump!' as her feet touch the floor. She then waits. Tina makes it happen again and again by moving forward to Ginny. She raises her arms to be lifted each time. As the routine is repeated, she adds a vocal sound, a high rising open vowel which sounds like the exaggerated 'and…'. After several repetitions, Wendy asks Ginny quietly, 'Is it worth waiting before "jump"?' All in the momentary gap between repetitions Ginny has answered 'Might be', and the next time they 'engineer' a pause just before the expected 'jump'. Tina says 'uh' in a very purposeful way as if trying to say the word, and Ginny responds instantly by giving her a particularly enthusiastic jump. They repeat the whole sequence several more times, now that Tina can use two distinct vocal sounds at different points in the game.

The musician's perspective

The music specialist has a relatively objective view of the whole process, and has experience of sessions with a range of staff, parents and children. Her intention is to use her voice and instrumental music to support and enhance the interaction as it happens, and to facilitate the sharing of power and control as appropriate.

She has introduced the familiar tune for 'Tap your feet', playing and singing it in time with Ginny's actions and words so as not to interrupt the flow. Knowing that the song lends itself to flexible use, she is always ready to sing a new verse more assertively if necessary, using actions that both Tina and other children have enjoyed in similar situations. However, she is primarily accompanying in this activity. She watches and listens to Ginny with intense concentration for any adjustments of timing, content or mood, in order to synchronise the music with precise moments of eye-contact, words or other communication. Having worked with the teacher for some time, Wendy recognises Ginny's particular cues – for example, she may slow down or get a little louder just before a deliberate pause.

Wendy tunes into and supports what she perceives as Ginny's and Tina's fluctuating levels of emotional arousal. She may also deliberately affect their moods, for example by playing a lively dance tune or a lullaby. In a more subtle way, she also marks Tina's eye-contact, vocalisation or physical approach with richer harmony or a different style of playing. She deliberately switches to the 'Row your boat' song, which has a rhythm more conducive to rocking than the previous tune, and tries to facilitate the shared movement with a flowing rhythmical accompaniment. She exaggerates the differences between the two contrasting actions, with loud 'tremolo' chords to build excitement at the wobble, and by playing the melody with gusto when Tina and Ginny 'row' vigorously.

As Tina and Ginny engage in the 'pre-verbal conversation', Wendy's contributions are finely tuned. She picks up the rhythm and pitch of each vocalisation and interprets it as a melodic phrase, playing and singing with Ginny in response to Tina. She also clarifies the turn-taking sequence by leaving a deliberate silence for the next contribution.

During the physical play routine, the musician accompanies and thereby seeks to enhance a game that is not essentially musical in nature. She uses a very common chord sequence and exaggerated vocal intonation to build tension on 'and …', resolving it on '…jump!' Once the routine is established, she can use the 'suspense' chord to help cue Tina in, picking up on any minute sign of intention. She observes that Tina is anticipating the 'jump', and intervenes verbally to give her the opportunity to request it intentionally.

Throughout the session, the musician takes an overview of the sharing of power within the interaction. She both accompanies and leads from the keyboard, depending on the moment-to-moment needs of the adult and child. She deliberately supports or even fills in a turn for both the adult and the child at various times, to keep the interaction flowing and maintain some degree of balance.

The teacher's perspective

In the particular situation described above the adult working with the child is a teacher. It should be noted here that this is not necessarily the case – the adult working with the child might be a parent or other adult. Importantly, however, that adult needs to know the child well. Ginny has worked with Tina daily in school for three months, both individually and in small groups. She brings her detailed knowledge of, and relationship with, Tina into the weekly music session. The episodes described above are just a few minutes in an ongoing long-term process: trust and mutual understanding have been built up gradually. Shared games and activities have been developed with great flexibility, often letting Tina take the lead, but gradually offering new activities and ideas. Ginny's primary motivation within the session is to engage Tina in mutually enjoyable shared play, in the knowledge that the child will be able to develop broader and more complex communication skills within this context. Although a casual observer might simply see an adult and child playing and having fun together, Ginny's role demands intense concentration and acute sensitivity, in order to keep Tina engaged and maximise her opportunities for communication.

As Ginny taps Tina's feet and playfully pulls her to the edge of the chair, she scans the child's face for feedback. She is aware that Tina sometimes finds intense close contact overwhelming, and is always ready to back away or simply avert her gaze slightly. Thus she instinctively regulates the level of emotional arousal: she can also build up excitement, extend a moment of anticipation, or deliberately calm down the activity. These strategies help Tina to stay involved in the interaction for as long as possible. Ginny also changes her position quickly to imitate Tina's brief independent foot-tapping within the song. She welcomes the spontaneous addition to Tina's repertoire of body actions, which has built up slowly, having been previously limited to rocking movements. It is also an opportunity to share an action with Tina, without any physical prompting or guidance. The familiar tune and action of the 'flexible' song acts as a kind of 'anchor' within the session, giving Ginny a context to try out new ideas as well as to follow Tina's lead. In this case it also gives her a framework in which to pursue one of her aims for Tina: to be more relaxed during physical contact.

Rocking cooperatively is not easy to achieve with Tina, and Ginny follows Wendy's lead in switching to the 'Row your boat' song, which has a natural rocking rhythm. She makes other subtle adjustments to enable Tina to be more relaxed, sensing the optimum speed and position through pressure of touch and weight transfer. As the pattern of wobbling on 'merrily' becomes established, Ginny exaggerates Tina's attempts to repeat the action, celebrating her intentional communication with lively activity and singing. Eventually the game peters out, when they are both too hot and tired to continue. At this natural break, Ginny stands back, with the intention of giving Tina (and perhaps herself) some physical and mental space after the intensity of the previous game. However, she makes it clear to Tina by her posture and responses that she is still available to play: she continues to watch and listen to her as she waits for whatever may happen next.

Ginny is instantly responsive to Tina's vocal sounds, knowing from previous sessions that imitating her is a good way to achieve shared attention and for Tina to experience imitative play, albeit on her own terms. She purposely responds to

Tina's unintentional sounds, enabling her to use them intentionally. Once the sequence is established, she initiates within it using Tina's own characteristic sounds, so that the roles are briefly reversed. She is clearly delighted by Tina's vocal response which is combined with looks and smiles. She recognises this moment of 'give and take' as a real step forward in the child's social communication development, knowing that over time she will begin to imitate and 'slot in' to frameworks, so that the power will be shared in a somewhat more balanced way.

Ginny is quick to respond to Tina's climbing on the chair as a potential attempt to request the 'jump' game. She has to interpret the rather passive response to her gestural and verbal offer of 'Jump?', but soon has a clearer cue from Tina. She continues the game with constant reference to what Tina does, showing obvious enthusiasm as her gesture and sounds become clearer and more assertive. Ginny agrees with Wendy's suggestion to wait before the key point, and does so in the spirit of wondering how Tina might ask for 'jump', rather than having a clear target behaviour. A look or movement would have been an adequate communication, but the distinct vocal sound is the best she could have hoped for, from a child who is as yet unable to use any words.

The child's perspective

Tina has been in school full-time for three months. Before this, despite the best efforts of her parents and various professionals, she was unable to make much sense of the things adults did and said, including their attempts to play with her. She was often fearful and withdrawn. She now knows what to expect in this situation, and in other regular sessions within the school routine. She seems to know that she can trust her individual worker to be sensitive to her needs and anxieties.

When Ginny picks up her feet and taps them together, she remains relaxed. Although she finds close contact overwhelming at times, this action within a familiar song is clearly a pleasant shared experience for her. The combined length of her legs and Ginny's arms also keeps the adult at a comfortable distance, which may be an important factor for natural eye-contact. When there is a sudden pause in the flow of the song, she sometimes makes fleeting eye-contact, perhaps initially out of surprise. She soon finds that when she does this, the game continues. She can also request another verse intentionally, by offering Ginny her feet. Thus she can communicate what she wants, and control how often and for how long the action continues.

As Ginny playfully pulls her off the chair towards her lap, Tina's first instinct is to re-position herself safely at the back of the chair. However, she wants the game to continue, and offers her feet again. She allows Ginny to pull her right off on the next repetition, and then appears to enjoy the 'bouncing' action, although her stiff back shows that she is now less relaxed. Neither is it easy for Tina to enter the flow of shared movement for 'Row the boat'. She could protest or get up and move away, but is clearly motivated enough to stay involved, and her body relaxes slightly. The familiar tune provides some security, and she begins to predict and anticipate the pattern of rocking and wobbling within the song. She finds she can make the 'wobble' happen over and over again, and becomes intensely involved in the energy and humour of this, apparently enjoying Ginny's surprise and exhaustion!

When given some 'space', Tina notices her reflection in the lens of the video camera, and makes some quiet vocal sounds at it. She responds immediately when Ginny repeats her own sounds gently back to her with musical accompaniment, and looks up, smiling, encouraged to try out more sounds. Her first 'snort' was probably not intended to be part of the game, but she finds it imitated and included in a simple sequence so that she *can* now repeat it intentionally. Tina is as yet unable to imitate speech sounds (or perhaps does not see the point of doing so), but by being imitated and then repeating her own sounds, she can now experience imitative play. The simple repetitive sequences enable her to predict Ginny's next sound, and she can even negotiate on a simple level to prolong the anticipation. She clearly finds it amusing to take part in this non-verbal conversation, and with the musical support she can stay involved for several turns.

When she climbs on the chair and looks round for Ginny, she is re-creating a game from a previous session. Since the adults recognise this as communication, she is able to initiate a social activity successfully. She clearly enjoys the feeling of being lifted and 'jumped', though her back is still rather stiff. Ginny's outstretched arms and a 'suspense' chord from the keyboard cue her in, but a gap after each 'jump' enables her to choose between repeating or not.

Within the simple structure of this jumping game, she first communicates through physical means, then adds vocal sounds. Once the game is flowing, she knows exactly how to get the action repeated, and is motivated to do it. Then a pause at the key point means she needs to request 'jump' specifically, and she finds a way to do so. Her emphatic vocal sound is very clearly intentional, and *in this context* easily understood by the adults. She thus experiences successful vocal communication as an integral part of a physical play routine.

By the end of the session described, Tina has been engaged almost continuously in shared play for over half an hour, and is happy to continue. She has found that her own specific sounds and movements can have immediate positive effects, and has begun to make sense of Ginny's actions, gestures, sounds, and maybe even some key words.

Discussion

Musical interaction sessions are largely about facilitating the development of communication skills in a social context. Finding shared social meaning may be difficult for those with autism, but this does not mean that we should abandon social learning and employ *only* compensatory strategies such as visual structure and clarification. Within Sutherland House School, where this approach has been developed (Christie and Wimpory 1986; Lewis *et al.* 1996), daily individual time with a key worker is mainly devoted to more conventional, though highly individualised, structured teaching. But once a week this time is used for a music session, putting social interaction and play firmly on the agenda.

Developing shared meaning – balancing predictability with flexibility

Ginny knows that, having been unable to make much sense of adults' social signals, Tina has been somewhat isolated during her preschool years. The teacher has gently but persistently found ways of entering *the child's* world in order to achieve shared play. In earlier sessions this involved joining in with her rocking at a distance, only very gradually attempting closer contact and developing more diverse actions. Tina is now willing and able to stay engaged for several minutes at a time, but Ginny still needs to 'tune in' closely to hold her attention and interest.

By this stage in her school life, Tina has given no clear evidence of verbal understanding, and in most situations cannot generally communicate her own needs and desires. In the music session, the activities are cultivated to make sense to her, even though she may not be driven by an active search for meaning. It provides a context in which she and Ginny are more likely to understand each other, so that she can see the pleasure in, and therefore learn through, the process of social interaction. She can make sense of some of Ginny's behaviour, and maybe even words, as the simple repetitive language is synchronised through the music with precise actions. The simple repetitive sequences in songs and games enable her to see a pattern in events, leading to moments of shared understanding. The musical framework helps to create and support those moments, so that Ginny can also understand what Tina wants in this context, even when her communication is not clear. Consequently both of them now often *predict* and anticipate what the other might do.

Jolliffe *et al.* (1992) describes the difficulty in predicting others' behaviour in a 'personal account' of autism:

> Objects are frightening... Moving objects are harder to cope with... Moving objects which also make a noise are even harder to cope with... Human beings are the hardest of all to understand... They move about when you are not expecting them to, they make varying noises and along with this, they place all kinds of demands on you which are just impossible to understand. As soon as you begin to think you are grasping how one of them works, something happens to change all this.

Part of Ginny's challenge, then, is to behave predictably enough for Tina to make sense of her actions, gestures, sounds and words. 'Hello' and 'Goodbye' songs are used consistently to frame each weekly session, and familiar sequences are built up in favourite songs and games. Episodes of these kinds of shared understanding enable Tina not only to anticipate favourite key moments, but with repetition eventually to communicate intentionally at these points.

Play routines like the 'And jump!' game allow a predictable pattern to be quickly established. These short repetitive shared games, also known as 'tension/expectancy games' (Nind and Hewett 1994) are extremely common in spontaneous play between adults and young children. They often involve active physical play, but their essence can be captured in activities adapted for all age groups and settings.

It is clearly vital for Tina to feel secure and be able to anticipate, if she is going to be an active partner in the social exchange. However, the adults involved do not intend to get drawn into extended rituals, which can be remembered purely by rote. They make sure that familiar activities are not always done in the same order, and will always be ready to develop and vary them in both planned and spontaneous ways. Even 'set' songs are therefore varied by contrasts in speed, volume, style of presentation, or an occasional change of order or content. Breaking that all-important predictability in small ways allows not only for real choices, but also for vital moments of teasing. This element of shared humour, based on a combination of timing skills and surprise, is very common in play with non-autistic infants, but often by-passes those with autism.

Flexibility within a structure is central to an interactive approach, enabling all the participants to be creative and to learn from each other. Jolliffe *et al.* (1992) suggests: 'There seems to be a trade-off between keeping the order the same to minimize fear and changing things to progress'. 'Flexible' action songs encapsulate this trade-off perfectly, by providing both a strong repetitive framework and infinite potential for variations in content, style and timing.

Enabling social learning

Some educationalists, in trying to adapt totally to an 'autistic' style of thinking, deliberately avoid social contexts for learning, in the belief that the child learns best through asocial methods. It may indeed be easier for a child with autism to learn some aspects of the curriculum through a computer program or by being guided physically from behind. However, facts and concepts learned in this way may remain for some children as disparate, disconnected pieces of knowledge.

Others simply miss the fact that children with autism have not developed the fundamental pre-verbal conversation skills which are the key to relationships and communication. They do not then provide the most helpful environment for learning and generalising. The key to social learning is in positive relationships with other people, and children with autism can and do make such relationships, given a conducive environment and adults who are persistent but sensitive in their attempts to 'build bridges'.

Some pre-verbal conversation skills which are of particular importance here are:

- Shared attention, which includes making eye-contact with another person and attending together to something else.
- Turn-taking, in the conversational sense, as opposed to the social rule of 'waiting for your turn'. Conversational turn-taking involves alternating your sounds and movements with someone else's, listening, watching and anticipating, using eye-contact to regulate the flow and a particular skill in 'social timing' (Newson 1978).

- Imitation, which young babies seem able to do with some facial movements from birth. Social imitation, however, with acknowledgement through looks and smiles, normally develops towards the end of the first year of life.
- Reciprocation, which describes that element of 'give and take' within interaction. It depends on both partners being willing and able to lead and respond in a flexible way, and brings a sense of balance to the conversation.

Play routines and songs can act as frameworks for interaction. Their use helps the adult to build up a repertoire of ideas to offer, and to structure and simplify her input – rather like Bruner's (1983) observation of how caregivers instinctively 'scaffold' early interaction, to facilitate the baby's communication. This facilitation also involves being very attentive and 'tuned-in' to the child, and attributing intention to sounds and movements.

Musical interaction (and other interactive approaches, such as Intensive Interaction, which is described in Chapter 4) deliberately sets out to re-create and exaggerate some key elements of early social play, to enable the development of those vital pre-verbal skills. As the child learns to attach meaning to the actions, gestures and words, so more complex ideas and concepts may develop naturally and be introduced intentionally. The approach can also be adapted as the child's verbal and cognitive ability increases. Many children with autism who are much more able and verbal than Tina still benefit from help in using fundamental conversational skills fluently and flexibly. In addition, a song can act as a framework for real verbal conversation, offering opportunities for introducing specific concepts and vocabulary, or for practising 'topic maintenance' and other elements of the art of conversation. Children with autism at more advanced stages of cognitive and language development may also benefit from extra support with imaginative play, enhanced by songs and musical accompaniment. The child's active involvement in the process creates an ideal context for learning new skills, and using them flexibly and creatively. The participating adult is also in an ideal relationship to help the child generalise and make connections, both within and outside the sessions.

Developing a sense of self

It may well be the case that babies learn about themselves through the process of interactive play with their parents and carers. The ways adults 'reflect back' and respond to spontaneous actions and sounds is particularly relevant to the development of a sense of agency (see Chapter 1), which in turn is vital for intentional communication.

Within the session described above, instant responses to Tina's vocal sounds increase her awareness of what she can do and how she can affect others. This is however quite a subtle process. *Exact* imitation of a child's sounds and actions is not only extremely difficult, but can lead to a degree of rigidity which is undesirable. Some children with autism can only be engaged by fairly close imitation in the early stages. However, the musical accompaniment enhances sounds and movements, and can highlight certain features. Stern (1985) points out that pure imitation reflects only shared behaviour, whereas capturing the essence of a movement, rhythm or sound by what he calls 'affect attunement' can actually express a shared feeling.

During a musical interaction session, the adults focus on, and keep written records of, the actual communicative acts which are visible and audible. But they are often conscious of something more profound happening in terms of emotions and the quality of the developing relationship. People with autism do not seem to develop awareness of their own and others' feelings in the same way as those without autism. It is impossible to know if and how far a pre-verbal child like Tina is aware of these aspects of self-development. Williams (1996) has written of a particular difficulty in processing 'self' and 'other' at the same time, an experience which, as she points out, is 'essential to grasping what "social" is, how to be it, and why you might want to be'. Tina is certainly discovering the powerful effects of her own communication, and in some ways is learning to integrate, or at least connect, her own experiences with those of another person. She may be acting mainly at the perceptual level as described by Stuart Powell in the opening chapter of this book; her initiation of a familiar game could be triggered by the room, the music, or simply by seeing a particular chair. She may not be aware of Ginny's feelings of enjoyment, surprise or doubt. Yet examples such as her flexible use of eye-contact and smiles in pre-verbal conversation, and her knowing repetition of 'merrily' in the song, indicate development that goes beyond the purely perceptual.

The role of the facilitator

In order to promote and nurture social learning, priority needs to be given to the quantity and quality of one-to-one 'teaching' time. This demands a high staff ratio and a degree of team-work within a school setting.

In the particular school in which the episodes described are set the music session is unique within the timetable in involving two adults to one child. The teacher who works with the child has detailed knowledge of, and an ongoing relationship with, the child. The musician observes and learns from a wide range of pairs – so that she becomes something of a 'specialist' despite her lack of direct contact with the children. (Within the school organisation, this lack of contact is recognised and compensated for by the music specialists' taking a full role at playtimes etc.) She regularly uses and suggests ideas and strategies learned during more established sessions to 'help along' an adult who is not used to working in this way, or to handle difficult moments.

The music specialist's role is specific to this approach. Although it is often compared with that of a music therapist, the dynamics and emphasis are essentially different. In musical interaction the musician's role is *not* to form a relationship with the child through the music (see Bunt 1994 for an explanation of music therapy), but to facilitate an adult who sees the child daily to do so, enabling immediate links with everyday situations. Having a third person who is outside the interaction in this sense is not essential to any of the individual activities, which may be repeated or indeed may have originated in other situations. Yet even with Ginny, who is highly skilled in this way of working, the finely timed musical input often enables the interaction to go on longer, and to develop in more intense and diverse ways. With less experienced staff, the music specialist may take on more of a 'coaching' role.

Apart from being almost universally enjoyed and therefore motivating, music can aid the interaction in specific ways. It can help to cue and mark alternating turns in conversational exchanges, emphasise rhythmic flow, create or enhance suspense and resolution, and bridge momentary gaps where the child's attention might otherwise be lost. The accompaniment also helps to make deliberate silences more salient, so that they can act as a cue. Nevertheless, many of the activities and strategies used in musical interaction are quite readily transferable to other settings. Someone who is not a musician, but is skilled in the communicative strategies, can successfully act in a similarly supportive role. For example, a speech and language therapist, preschool support worker or school 'outreach' teacher may facilitate interactive play between a child and parent or a member of staff (Christie and Prevezer 1998).

An interactive approach

At Sutherland House School where these episodes took place, a musical interaction session is a relatively short but important part of the child's week. It takes place alongside, and is partially integrated with, both speech and language therapy input and the teaching curriculum. This curriculum, of course, includes the full range of subjects, adapted as appropriate for both individuals and groups.

The approach might be described as both therapeutic and educational. It aims to remediate some of the core difficulties faced by the child with autism in relation to his/her functioning in the social world. There is little overt 'teaching' in the traditional sense, yet the session is extremely rich in terms of learning. All three participants are learning to find points of contact and ways of communicating with others who do not see things in the same way as themselves. In addition to practising pre-verbal skills and beginning to make connections concerning the use and understanding of actual words, Tina is learning that interacting can be fun, is worthwhile in its own right, and is not always difficult. She is learning that she can affect others' behaviour in a positive way by taking an active part in shared games. She is also surely getting the message that she is 'good to be with': as Nind and Hewett (1994) point out, motivation and a sense of well-being are central to progress in social communication.

In an interactive approach, by definition, the child's spontaneous actions and sounds are allowed to affect what the adult does or says next. Non-directive techniques such as joining in, copying sounds, or singing a running commentary, can all draw a child in to shared play, convey acceptance, and help to build confidence. Allowances must be made for individual sensitivities: a degree of subtlety may be needed for one child and dramatic exaggeration for another. Such an approach is not totally non-directive, though the child may need to take the lead for some time in order to stay involved voluntarily. This could be for anything from a few minutes to several months of weekly sessions. However, ultimately the aim is for a social relationship of negotiation and balance, where both partners make choices, and respond to and initiate communication.

Many episodes within the session described follow behavioural principles within the interactive framework. However, the interaction is *not* restricted to the sequence of 'stimulus – response – feedback' which is the hallmark of a behavioural approach. For example, Ginny pauses in a familiar sequence, and continues when Tina responds. In this way, eye-contact and vocal sounds are 'reinforced'. However, she also keeps the song or game flowing, using rewards that are both social and intrinsic to the activity. While feedback and praise are given naturally after a successful episode, Ginny does not interrupt the flow of the game with frequent phrases such as 'good girl' or 'well done'. This reflects the vital principle that the *process* of interaction is given as much value as, if not more than, the product. Interactive sessions are by no means aimless, but they are not led by pre-set targets.

Implications for teaching

- Children with autism *can* learn socially, but need to be shown that it is worthwhile, and how to do it. The skills that adults draw on intuitively when interacting with young babies are relevant and adaptable to teaching older children with autism. Facilitating effective social learning may involve re-defining 'teaching' to a certain extent.
- We have to *make* social experiences and language meaningful for children who are not driven by an active search for meaning. An interactive approach promotes quality relationships, helping children to understand, to make connections, and to generalise.
- It is vital to address the conversational skills which underpin language and communication development. When shared attention, turn-taking, imitation and reciprocation become everyday habits, children can learn more from those around them.
- Musical Interaction can provide contexts which are familiar and motivating, helping a child and adult to make sense of each other so that new information and ideas may be more easily learned and understood.
- The most effective rewards for communication are those which are *intrinsic* to the activity. Successful communication is self-perpetuating: over-dependence on frequent verbal praise interrupts the flow of interaction.
- Humour, suspense, excitement and emotional warmth are essential elements in interactive work and play, but levels of emotional arousal always need careful regulation, taking into account the preferences and sensitivities of each child.

- Flexibility and balance are vital within interactions. The challenge and the rich rewards of an interactive approach stem from having to combine instinct and intuition with an understanding of the processes of early communication development.

This chapter has attempted to illustrate how an interactive approach can complement more conventionally structured teaching. The experiences described suggest that working in this way may prove beneficial to relationships, communication and learning, both within and beyond the school context.

Acknowledgement

The author wishes to acknowledge the help given by Phil Christie and Di Saville in commenting on drafts of the chapter.

References

Bruner, J. (1983) *Child's Talk: Learning to Use Language*. Oxford: Oxford University Press.

Bunt, L. (1994) *Music Therapy: An Art Beyond Words*. London: Routledge.

Christie, P. and Prevezer, W. (1998) *Interactive Play*. Ravenshead: Early Years Diagnostic Centre*.

Christie, P. and Wimpory, D. (1986) 'Recent research into the development of communicative competence and its implications for the teaching of autistic children', *Communication* **20**(1), 4–7.

Jolliffe, T., Lansdowne, R. and Robinson, C. (1992) 'Autism: a personal account', *Communication* **26**(3).

Lewis, R., Prevezer, W. and Spencer, R. (1996) *Musical Interaction: An Introduction*. Ravenshead: Early Years Diagnostic Centre.

Newson, E. (1978) *Making Sense of Autism*. Ravenshead: Early Years Diagnostic Centre.

Nind, M. and Hewett, D. (1994) *Access to Communication*. London: David Fulton Publishers.

Stern, D. (1985) *The Interpersonal World of the Infant*. New York: Basic Books.

Williams, D. (1996) *Autism – An Inside-Out Approach*. London: Jessica Kingsley Publishers.

* *Note:* The Early Years Diagnostic Centre runs its own non-profit making Information Service. Its documents that are cited in this chapter are available by mail order from the Centre at 272 Longdale Road, Ravenshead, Nottinghamshire NG15 9AH.

Chapter Six

Autism and Family Therapy: A Personal Construct Approach

Harry Procter

Introduction

The family is the first arena in which we develop as persons and learn to relate. A person with autism has a specific difficulty in communicating and relating to others and this initially becomes apparent in family interaction early in the child's life. This can be a devastating discovery for parents and other family members. It is of vital importance to work with the family to address the child's needs as early as possible, to support the other members and to help the family optimise the learning environment for the child.

In many ways, working with the child in the context of the family is the ideal setting to help them make progress in overcoming the difficulties associated with autism, to the extent that this is possible. The person with autism will necessarily be dependent to a lesser or greater extent on a group of carers, usually family members. In the family the opportunity and necessity is there for the child with autism to learn how to relate to those closest to him or her effectively, as well as for them to relate in turn to him or her. The family therapy session becomes, in the most supportive manner, a 'laboratory' for looking at the way autism affects ongoing communication and relationships, by therapist and family reflecting on episodes of their difficult and successful experiences, making sense of what is happening and how to respond to it.

Family therapy has developed in the context of an approach called 'systems theory'. There is a large literature and many trends within this tradition (e.g. Dallos and Draper 1999) but so far not much has appeared about autism. Morgan (1988), Konstantareas (1990) and Norton and Drew (1994) have written useful papers, however, and Vetere (1993) and Fiddell (1996) have written good introductions to systemic work with learning disabilities in general.

There is, of course, a long tradition of helping families through behavioural and educational techniques (e.g. Leisten 1997; Estrada and Pinsof 1995; Howlin 1998) which can be readily assimilated into systemic family work. These emphasise the importance of structured programmes, communication through visually presented materials (Schopler 1997) and making the child's choices and initiatives central (Bondy and Frost 1996; Manolson 1992). While we are discussing literature, there are also excellent materials written for parents and siblings (e.g. Attwood 1998; Schopler 1995; Howlin 1998; Davies 1994) and it is useful to have these on hand to show and lend to family members.

Anyone working with autism needs to have a good knowledge of the condition itself or there may be a danger of underestimating what a serious disability it is or attributing it to 'poor parenting', 'family dysfunction' or to the interaction patterns themselves. Of course, the families will also have their fair share, like any other family, of stress, conflicts, and of experiences such as bereavement, separation and divorce, stepfamily issues, mental health problems with which the family therapist will try and help them. The autism itself, however, remains the result of impairment of the development of the central nervous system, perhaps affecting the amygdala, the frontal and temporal lobes. A higher proportion has other organic problems such as epilepsy, and three quarters of those diagnosed with autism have learning disabilities. Having a family member with autism is usually extremely stressful, it may severely restrict family life for the foreseeable future and radically alter the course and experience of the family's life (Schopler and Mesibov 1984).

The systemic approach emphasises that all behaviour occurs in a social context and that there are different levels of contexts. One cannot look at behaviour in isolation from others' reactions in the ongoing interaction. The behaviour of a child with autism will vary greatly between the contexts of home, school, when out and about and when in the clinic setting. For example a six-year-old boy, James, is very good at school and very naughty with his dad at home, but if his mum is present he tends to be easier for his father to deal with. Things do not escalate into father shouting and James having tantrums associated with his routines so much when she is there. We can think of the routines in isolation, but the systemic view encourages us to look at the patterns of interaction within which the routines, shouting and tantrums occur. Kozloff (1984) describes these patterns as 'structured exchanges'.

The personal construct approach

Personal construct psychology (Kelly 1955) is a well-known approach within psychology and psychotherapy. Kelly's system was one of the first comprehensive cognitive models of human functioning and his work has been influential within clinical psychology (Winter 1992), educational psychology (Ravenette 1999), speech and language therapy (Hayhow and Levy 1989), and counselling (Fransella and Dalton 1990). My own work has involved applying personal construct psychology (PCP) to working with families with child and adult mental health problems (Procter 1981, 1985, 1996). This can be counted as a systemic approach to family therapy but has a much more elaborate psychology of individual functioning, which will prove particularly useful when we consider autism.

PCP starts with the basic assumption that everybody has a unique view of the world that is apprehended through a finite number of personal constructs. The person uses these to construe their situation and anticipate events. Every-day concepts such as *happy, violent* or *close* take on unique meanings and connotations in the person's life experience. These constructs are two-ended, allowing discriminations to be made (this boy is *friendly*, because he is smiling, whereas that girl looks *stroppy*). There is always a choice to be made between two options. Kelly assumes that we have genuinely free choices, although constrained at any one time by the streets and avenues of our construct system.

The construct system gradually evolves as individuals develop in early social interaction with others. It has a hierarchical nature. One construct, e.g. 'smiling', is personal evidence for a more abstract, or *superordinate* construct such as 'friendly' which in its turn defines smiling (Figure 6.1). Also 'friendly' ('I feel friendly') comes to *govern* or *channelise* the choice or act of smiling. The constructs at different levels are in *ordinal relationship* to each other. The system of constructs, with many layers, has a pyramidal shape, with the core constructs at the top. Core constructs govern our lives across the different contexts and may provide a sense of self. For example, one person may have core construing based on Christian values (I aim to be 'kind to others'), another may use scientific ideas (I just want the 'objective truth'). The construct system governs both the way we see the world and the way we act within it.

The therapist takes an interest in, and pays particular attention to, the constructs family members use as these structure the way people tackle their difficulties. This helps us to understand how they proceed and allows us to be relevant to them. To see Tom as 'doing it to get back at me' as opposed to 'he can't help it' leads to an entirely different approach to Tom, feeling angry with him rather than sympathetic. A small change in construing can therefore lead to larger changes in daily interactions. The personal construct therapist helps the family elaborate their

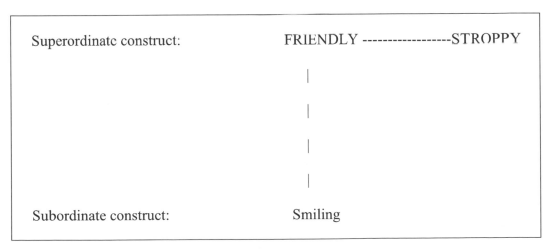

Superordinate construct: FRIENDLY -----------------STROPPY

Subordinate construct: Smiling

Figure 6.1 The hierarchical connection of constructs

understandings and revise their approaches whilst accepting and working within their existing, superordinate beliefs.

Through detailed conversations with the family a set of beliefs and competences will emerge, their construing having evolved over years of family life and traditions arising from their parents' culture, religion, extended family and so on. These provide the ability to cope and generate ideas that so many families are able to demonstrate, once they have a better understanding of what they are dealing with. On the other hand, therapists may encounter family members with very restricted ways of construing their situation. This may well relate to them being affected by autism themselves, given the significant genetic loading for autism. This is more likely to occur in the males than in the female members. Therapists will still usually need to work within their construing, which can be extremely challenging and requires great patience. Howlin (1998) recounts a case of a father who obsessionally re-presented the children's food if they had failed to finish it during the previous meal. Howlin utilised the father's [autistic] tendency to ignore his son's tantrums, persuading him to do the same with the unfinished meals.

Personal construct psychology and autism

As a rich theory of human cognition, PCP is able to give a detailed and integrated account of autistic spectrum disorders (Procter, unpublished paper). We would normally expect the child to gradually develop a more and more elaborate set of constructs through childhood as more situations and fields of knowledge are encountered and construed, these becoming more hierarchical with time (Livesley and Bromley 1973). In autism there seems to be a basic difficulty in ordinal relationships being formed between the constructs. Mottron *et al.* (1999) refer to this as a *hierarchisation deficit.* There is a problem with putting features together into a coherent whole (Frith 1989; Happé 1998). The result is a fragmented view of the world in which the 'big picture' is not recognised. Instead, the child will notice small features that have changed that the rest of the family will miss, and he or she may be overwhelmed by a mass of incidental stimuli.

Ordinal relationships between constructs are essential for normal comprehension. Language is classically structured hierarchically (phoneme–word–sentence–story) and a lack of being able to put things into context will severely disrupt comprehension, communication and imagination. Most crucially though, it leads to difficulties in being able to understand another's point of view or in PCP terms to *subsume* another way of construing. Kelly (1955) put this ability at the centre of our being able to relate in his *sociality corollary:* 'To the extent that one person construes the construction processes of another, he or she may play a role in a social process involving the other person' (p. 95). A 'mindblindness' is now widely regarded as being a central impairment in autism (Baron-Cohen 1997). Baron-Cohen sees the problem as a delay rather than a basic inability. Tests of the ability to construe *primary* ('Sally thinks the marble is in the basket') and *secondary* ('Mary thinks that John thinks the ice-cream van is in the park') representations may be passed later by the child with autism, (e.g. at 7-years-old instead of 4 years and perhaps 12-years-old instead of 7 years). This kind of conception of developmental progression may lead to a more optimistic view as to the extent to which the children with autism can make progress in this area.

Problems with sociality lead to severe and pervasive disruptions of social interaction in the family and particularly with the peer group, where allowances may not be made for the child's difficulties. Difficulties with joint referencing or 'secondary intersubjectivity' (Trevarthen and Hubley 1978) make it hard for the child to participate in the business of building a shared system of constructs in the family in which it is understood what the significance of objects and events have for each member. It also leads to a difficulty in being able to reflect on one's own constructions, one result being a difficulty with remembering personal experiences (Powell and Jordan 1995). In this sense the children will have little ability to comprehend their own role in the family system.

Having a construct system which is lacking in hierarchical organisation, fragmented into unrelated meanings and unable to subsume other's constructions leaves the child with a difficulty in anticipating events, particularly social events such as the expressions, gestures, cues and tones of voice which indicate emotional meanings (Hobson 1993). At a more macro level, the child will not appreciate situations and people's parts in the drama of life as it unfolds. This is likely to lead to intense anxiety and frustration, or alternatively an absence of interest in the social world. It may lead to the child becoming extremely dominating, in order to restore a sense of predictability. For example, one child with Asperger's syndrome whom I visited recently insisted on his mother, sister (and me) participating in his game of digging for bones in the garden and playing lifeguards with his ear-piercing whistles, of which he has a large collection. Insistence on routines, intolerance of change, stereotyped behaviours and elaborate circumscribed interests may all develop in autism to make the world more tolerable to live in, given that understanding of the social world is precluded to a greater or lesser extent.

The process of therapy with the family

Family therapy with autism involves of a series of phases or tasks, which usually need addressing. I will typically work with a family for 10 to 15 sessions over a period of months, with offers of telephone contact during and after this period. Different family members attend the sessions as appropriate: the child or young person with autism, the parents, siblings, grandparents, and members of the professional network.

A diagnosis may already have been made but usually, in my experience, a child is often referred where people have begun to suspect autism or Asperger's syndrome but it is not yet confirmed. This situation obviously needs sensitive handling. One of the particular difficulties of autism is the way it usually only insidiously becomes noticeable during infancy. It is bad enough when parents discover serious disability in their child at birth, but to have thought that the child is developing normally and then find that he/she has a profound and lifelong condition such as autism can be a particularly cruel blow. Parents are prone to searching self-blame or accusations of blame by members of the extended family, or by a partner.

If parents agree, the whole family usually attends the first session, allowing us all to get to know one another. A telephone call will have established the parent's choice about who to bring to the session. This usually takes place in a clinic setting which is child-friendly with toys and drawing materials. This initial interview (typically one-and-a-half hours) serves to begin the development of a therapeutic alliance, with an emphasis on strengths and interests, about their lives, for example about schools and work, what support they have from extended family and others. The children are kept centre stage, leaving material that could be uncomfortable until an interview where the parents attend alone. Realistic goals may be set and these are stated in a way that the child and the siblings will understand as far as is possible given their developmental stage.

Therapists will encounter many forms of family including those containing single parents, divorcing parents, stepfamilies, and families where child protection issues exist. Sensitivity to gender, race and culture is central in this work. Women may typically bear the main brunt of care and often feel overwhelmed, isolated and disempowered. It is important to establish what the constructions of 'disability' are in the subculture (White 1997).

Issues concerning diagnosis

Any family has developed a family construct system (Procter 1996), with rich narratives about relationships, child development, what parenting involves, how to deal with difficult behaviour and house rules. However, these do not necessarily equip them for the enormous and complex task of bringing up a child with autism. Constructs about children, probably even before they are conceived, will be in place. Certainly when they are born they may very quickly become construed as similar to or different from other relatives: 'He's just like his grandad!' The family may develop an investment in a particular path for the child and it is not at all easy to accept that expectations may not always be met. Accepting a diagnosis involves a huge shift in the family construct system, with radical shifts not only in how the child concerned is construed, but in all the associated roles and relationships.

The diagnostic process itself will be therapeutic if done thoroughly and appropriately. Going through structured interviews such as the ADI-R (Lord *et al.* 1994) with the parents, in which many detailed examples of the child's development and behaviour are examined, is a useful process in both educational and therapeutic terms. The parents will gain a better and more detailed understanding of their child's difficulties. This process is likely to be emotional, with feelings of loss and anxiety about the future. In my practice the diagnostic phase will be prefaced by an explanation of autism with plenty of time for clarification and questions. This helps the parents become genuine collaborators in the process. A home visit and observations at playgroup or school are conducted. The reports of paediatricians, psychologists, speech and language therapists and others are studied.

In the family work, the next sessions will involve joining the parents in making sense of their child's difficulties, discussing how to manage situations and promoting an optimum learning situation for the child's, or young person's, development. What the therapist is working with at any point is parents' constructions of what autism is, not his/her own idea of it. Family members will be heavily influenced by the way they see and feel about the particular child, their construction of their lives as a whole and their cultural and religious beliefs.

When the diagnosis of an autistic spectrum disorder has been clarified, the parents will usually know how to explain this to other family members appropriately. Siblings and others may attend the sessions. Explaining autism in simple terms and throwing light on particular problematic situations in terms of theory can be enormously helpful for them, but it may also be painful. Explaining the difficulties to the child with autism him/herself is an important consideration. Parents may prefer to do this themselves, as natural opportunities for the conversation arise. They typically find some good ways of doing this. The books for siblings (e.g. Davies 1994) are useful here. An eight-year-old with Asperger's syndrome, initially reluctant to look at the book, ended up devouring it avidly through to the end. Some parents prefer the professional to talk to the child. The child as a person with strengths should of course be emphasised as a context to explanations about difficulties and related to examples of the child's experiences. How to do this obviously depends on the child's cognitive level and the level of autism in terms of the capacity to self-reflect.

Occasionally, the diagnosis itself will lead to improvements in behaviour as approaches made to situations are better tuned to the child's difficulties, preventing escalation into conflict or frustration and blame. But the family is faced with the situation of typically extreme difficulties that can be expected to remain with them for the foreseeable future. The challenge of the therapy is to help the family to gradually enable the child or young person to find ways of addressing their own impairments and difficulties.

Addressing constructs governing social hierarchy

The hierarchy or differences in power within the family are often of central concern to the therapist. Paradoxically the child with autism is often the most dominating member with parents feeling like slaves, organised around the child's needs and demands. Common means of influence, for example behavioural techniques of charting and giving social praise, may be reduced in effect. The construct model looks at power relations in the context of the constructs being applied by each participant.

An example of how we might construe a situation is of five-year-old Andrew, mentioned earlier, who dominates the household with his games that he expects his family to play continuously. We can draw a so-called 'bow-tie' diagram (Procter 1985) of what happens (Figure 6.2). He demands that his mother put certain clothing on and come into the garden to dig for bones (Andrew's *action*) and she feels that she has to go along with him or he'll have a tantrum (mother's *construct*). This governs her actions in perpetuating the pattern, keeping Andrew within a predictable social experience but with him in charge and with his mother feeling powerless. This model of how the relationship is working sees choices (between the bipolar options) existing within a system that constrains or entraps the participants (Procter and Parry 1978).

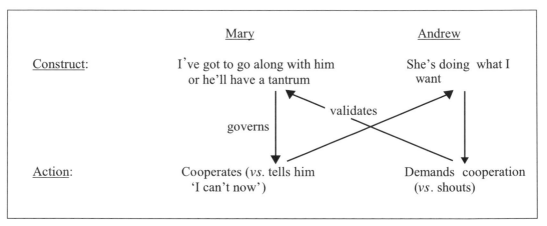

Figure 6.2 'Bow-tie' of the structured exchange between Andrew and his mother

The first task for the therapist is to gather the sort of information in the diagram through conversation and questioning, considering particular situations in detail and if possible observing the way they operate in practice. This process itself serves to get the family to reflect on their own experience in detail. It may be very difficult to establish how the child is construing and we will need to make informed guesses from the context and see if these fit the actual situation.

These patterns may have an escalatory quality, culminating in aggression or punishment, or they may have a stable continual quality. Family members may be aware of the pattern but it is helpful to have it articulated in words and diagrams. Existing attempted solutions by family members tend to be directed at different parts of the structured exchange, for example explaining to Andrew (an attempt to change his construct), sending him to his room (changing his action), refusing to do it (choosing the contrast pole of the mother's construct) or getting angry (contrast of the mother's action).

The pattern itself may become the focus of therapy. One couple I was working with described themselves as either driving these patterns (around their daughter's nightly three-hourly routine) and forcing the pace, or hanging back. As their daughter procrastinated in eating, doing her homework and her piano practice, they could slacken off but she would 'go ballistic' if a part of the routine was omitted. By thinking of the pattern of the structured exchange as a whole, the therapist can enable the family members to begin to get back into control of it and gradually modify it. This may take weeks or months, but to continue to react (in an uncontrolled way) tends to perpetuate it.

Howlin (1998) has shown how significant progress with stereotyped and ritualistic behaviours can be made through the graded change approach. Here, paradoxically, the routine is accepted but small step-changes are made in modifying them, such as changing where they occur, how many times, the duration, or who is involved. Erickson was the first to take this approach when he was working with such problems as enuresis, habit disorders and obsessions. He describes a case of a man who *had to* urinate through a wooden tube. Erickson had him cut a tiny piece off the tube each week, until eventually he could make do with just his hand as a 'tube' (Erickson 1980).

In a similar way, we can make small changes to any one of the four components in the structured exchange, although the child's construct may not be open to direct influence. Changes can be made in the parents' action (for example, changing location, pace, scheduling in time, partial reinforcement, distraction, changing the style of cooperating). Studying the diagram itself may help the parents to change their approach and frame the child's action with 'I must not go along with this behaviour because I am only perpetuating it in the long term.' In this particular example, Andrew's parents returned to the following session saying that the situation had moved on significantly, with Mary feeling empowered to assert herself in a manner Andrew accepted.

Adrian: developing sociality

A central aspect of the disorder of autism is a problem with using some constructs to subsume others. In the family, the lack of the child's ability to empathise or construe the other members' signals and points of view is deeply problematic for all concerned. In general, the essence of construct oriented family therapy is to increase understanding or sociality between the members. The conversation of the session will naturally increase mutual understanding as family members negotiate the meaning of their own experiences.

The therapist carefully helps family members to articulate their constructions as much as possible. He or she pauses the flow of conversations to check that the child understood, 'What did Mum want? How did Dad feel? He was happy wasn't he, he was smiling!' In this way the family learn that it is necessary to spell out what is normally taken for granted in interchanges. This must not rely too much on the verbal. Drawings, diagrams and re-plays are extremely helpful here. The bow-tie, in Figure 6.2, is particularly helpful in talking about understanding the other's construct in a situation. Howlin *et al.* (1999) have produced a nice volume of pictured situations in which the child has to guess whether the person was feeling happy, sad, angry or frightened. We can apply the same method to particular situations arising in the family.

Many basic personal construct questioning methods are helpful in deepening our understanding of the child with autism's constructions. The following example shows how questions may reveal where the young person's thinking is falling short of being useful for anticipation and participation in interaction.

Adrian's family had been in considerable conflict for many years. His mother was continually criticised by her partner and her older son for pampering Adrian, who had an obsession playing with Barbie Dolls when younger. They didn't like the way he spoke in an effeminate manner and felt she was encouraging him to do this. The first part of the therapy involved a diagnosis of Asperger's syndrome. The family atmosphere improved significantly as the others accepted that this was an appropriate way of describing his difficulties and the previous patterns of blame were modified. His mother later said that they would have split up if they had carried on as before. Adrian's stepfather became kinder to him although his older brother remained distant, not really accepting the diagnosis.

My work with the family was mainly through Adrian coming with his mother, although Adrian would not always agree to come. Adrian now had a special interest in Hollywood movies and knew all the facts associated with the directors and could quote from film magazines verbatim. He would talk about this at great length but he would first ask his mother's permission if he could talk about films.

I asked Adrian, a delightful lad of 13, what three things he could think of that were positive about him. He said 'intelligent', 'a good film designer' and 'good memory for films'. We explored these ideas together with the contrast poles, listing examples of different poles. 'What would not being intelligent involve?' Asked, are there any negative ways someone could describe him, he said, 'no, nothing'. His Mum answered the question about his three best aspects with, 'He's *caring, loving* and *polite.*' I asked him if he knew why she said that about him, and in what ways, and so on.

In another session we talked about his friends. His mother made clear that in no way could they be classed as 'friends' but I went on to ask Adrian in what way two of the three – Tim, Sheila and Pete – were similar and the other one different (known as the triad method of eliciting a construct). He said Tim and Pete have the same interests and Sheila is 'off me' and 'angry at times'. He said Sheila 'turns awfully different', for example when she left him at the side of the road. This poignantly indicates, perhaps, how people may be construed in the autistic experience. Clearly more than one construct has appeared here, but it is all useful material for exploring his world. His mother said to me, 'This is very interesting: you speak to him differently to me. It reveals the difficulties and misunderstandings he has with relationships.'

Constructs can be combined together in a table known as the 'repertory grid technique' (Fransella and Bannister 1977; Beail 1985). These are quite time consuming but reveal rich data and can be computer analysed to give an aggregated picture of the person's construing. They were used to look at mothers' construing of learning disabled one-year-olds (Vicary 1985). Hare *et al.* (1999) in a recent grid study of adults with Asperger's syndrome argue that the grid is specially suitable for these clients with their preference for formal structures, external cues and an interest in number, order and sequence. Hare (1997) claims successful use with people with IQs of 50+.

A simple qualitative grid I like to use with families is the Perceiver Element grid or PEG (Procter 1996). Perceivers are on the left (see Figure 6.3) and how they see each member or 'element' is entered in the appropriate cell. Adrian sees his brothers as 'a pain in the bum' and a 'complete pain'. Adrian and his mother helped me fill such a grid out to look at the interpersonal perceptions amongst his family. Words or pictures can be put in the cells. This is particularly valuable as it allows items from the conversational flow to be put in a diagram. One can then point to it and explain agreements and disagreements (e.g. both you and your stepdad think Sue is 'lovely': you *agree* with him). Getting him to wonder 'What would your sister say about your elder brother?' may focus his mind. Or his mother might help. We can get him to ask her. The discourse of sociality is encouraged and introduced into the family's daily life.

		Elements:				
		Adrian	Mother	Brother (19)	Brother (16)	Niece
	Adrian			Pain in the bum	Complete pain	Lovely, gorgeous
	Mother		Totally stressed, non-approachable			
Perceivers:	Stepdad					Lovely, sweet
	Brother (19)	Complete pain				
	Sister	Not worrying about me as much				

Figure 6.3 Perceiver Element grid in Adrian's family
(Note: rows and columns are included in this grid only where they contain material)

Another method for looking at superordinate constructs, is called 'laddering'. I asked Adrian about his first self-construct *intelligent vs. not intelligent.* Which would he rather be? He said 'intelligent'. I asked why. He said, 'it helps me learn things' (vs. 'hard to learn things'). Figure 6.4 shows how the 'rungs' of the ladder can be built up from the original construct by asking why he would prefer to be the alternative. His highest construct 'it would be eventful' is interesting, and perhaps gives us an insight into why films appeal to him so much. His head is full of bits from the films and snippets of critical comment from film magazines.

These methods, used in the course of the family session, are valuable for focusing the members' minds on personal meanings and their capacity to successfully understand each other's positions. This will empower them to understand their family member with autism better and to deal very concretely and specifically when misunderstandings and inability to understand arise, in the context of the particular family meanings in question.

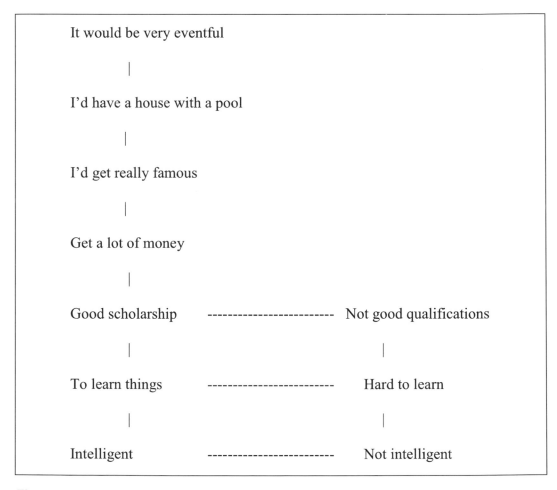

Figure 6.4 Ladder of Adrian's constructs

Conclusion

Personal construct psychology not only provides a set of techniques or therapeutic methods but also gives us a framework for understanding and discussing human change processes. Its language and methods can be used to describe the changes that occur in other types of therapeutic intervention such as behaviour therapy, creative and educational approaches or any type of approach to autism. It looks at the whole family and the ways the members mark out their worlds. *Their* model is potentially far more usable and relevant to them ultimately than frameworks we may seek to impose. Most are, of course, only too eager to devour any ideas from the literature we may be able to provide them with, but they will make their own sense of these and integrate them into their family construct systems.

References

Attwood, A. (1998) *Asperger's Syndrome*. London: Jessica Kingsley.

Baron-Cohen, S. (1997) *Mindblindness*. London: MIT Press.

Beail, N. (1985) *Repertory Grid Technique and Personal Constructs*. Beckenham: Croom Helm.

Bondy, A. and Frost, L. (1996) 'Educational approaches in pre-school', in Schopler, E. and Mesibov, G. (eds) *Learning and Cognition in Autism*. New York: Plenum Press.

Dallos, R. and Draper, R. (1999) *An Introduction to Family Therapy*. Milton Keynes: The Open University.

Davies, J. (1994) *Children with Autism: A Booklet for Brothers and Sisters*. Nottingham University: Early Years Centre.

Erickson, M. H. (1980) *Innovative Hypnotherapy*. New York: Irvington.

Estrada, A. U. and Pinsof, W. M. (1995) 'The effectiveness of family therapies for selected behavioural disorders of childhood', *Journal of Marital and Family Therapy* **21**(4), 403–40.

Fiddell, B. (1996) 'Making family therapy user-friendly for learning disabled clients', *Context* 26, 11–13.

Fransella, F. and Bannister, D. (1977) *A Manual for Repertory Grid Technique*. London: Academic Press.

Fransella, F. and Dalton, P. (1990) *Personal Construct Counselling in Action*. New York: Sage.

Frith, U. (1989) *Autism: Explaining the Enigma*. Oxford: Blackwell.

Happé, F. (1998) 'Psychological accounts of non-social assets and deficits in autism', paper given at National Autistic Society Conference, Hammersmith, London.

Hare, D. J. (1997) 'Use of repertory grid techniques in working with people with learning disabilities', *Journal of Learning Disabilities for Nursing, Health and Social Care* **1**(3), 115–19.

Hare, D. J., Jones, J. P. R. and Paine, C. (1999) 'Approaching reality: the use of personal construct assessment in working with people with Asperger's syndrome', *Autism* **3**(2), 165–76.

Hayhow, R. and Levy, C. (1989) *Working with Stuttering: A Personal Construct Therapy Approach*. Bicester: Winslow.

Hobson, R. P. (1993) *Autism and the Development of Mind*. Hove: Lawrence Erlbaum.

Howlin, P. (1998) *Children with Autism and Asperger's Syndrome*. Chichester: Wiley.

Howlin, P., Baron-Cohen, S. and Hadwin, J. (1999) *Teaching Children with Autism to Mind-read*. Chichester: Wiley.

Kelly, G. A. (1955) *The Psychology of Personal Constructs*, Vols. 1 and 2. New York: Norton. (Second edition, 1991. London: Routledge and Kegan Paul)

Konstantareas, M. M. (1990) 'A psychoeducational model for working with families of autistic children', *Journal of Marital and Family Therapy* **16**(1), 59–70

Kozloff, M. A. (1984) 'A training program for families of children with autism', in Schopler, E. and Mesibov, G. B. (eds) *The Effects of Autism on the Family*. New York: Plenum Press.

Leisten, R. (1997) 'Parenting learning disabled children', in Dwivedi, K. N. (ed.) *Enhancing Parenting Skills*. London: Wiley.

Livesley, W. and Bromley, D. B. (1973) *Person Perception in Children and Adolescents*. Chichester: Wiley.

Lord, C., Rutter, M. and LeCouteur, A. (1994) 'Autism diagnostic interview–revised', *Journal of Autism and Developmental Disorders* **24**, 659–86.

Manolson, A. (1992) *It Takes Two to Talk*. Toronto: The Hanen Centre.

Morgan, S. B. (1988) 'The autistic child and family functioning: A developmental-family systems perspective', *Journal of Autism and Developmental Disorders* **18**(2), 263–80.

Mottron, L., Belleville, S. and Ménard, E. (1999) 'Local bias in autistic subjects as evidenced by graphic tasks: Perceptual hierarchisation or working memory deficit?', *Journal of Child Psychology and Psychiatry* **40**(5), 743–55.

Norton, P. and Drew, C. (1994) 'Autism and potential family stressors', *American Journal of Family Therapy* **22**(1), 67–76.

Powell, S. D. and Jordan, R. R. (1995) *Understanding and Teaching Children with Autism*. Chichester: Wiley.

Procter, H. G. (1981) 'Family construct psychology: An approach to understanding and treating families', in Walrond-Skinner, S. (ed.), *Developments in Family Therapy*. London: Routledge.

Procter, H. G. (1985) 'A construct approach to family therapy and systems intervention', in Button, E. (ed.) *Personal Construct Theory and Mental Health*. Beckenham: Croom Helm.

Procter, H. G. (1996) 'The family construct system', in Kalekin-Fishman, D. and Walker, B. (eds) *The Construction of Group Realities*. Malabar: Krieger.

Procter, H. G. (unpublished paper) Personal construct psychology and autism', paper submitted to the *Journal of Constructivist Psychology*.

Procter, H. G. and Parry, G. (1978) 'Constraint and freedom: The social origin of personal constructs', in Fransella, F. (ed.) *Personal Construct Psychology 1977*. London: Academic Press.

Ravenette, A. T. (1999) *Personal Construct Theory in Educational Psychology*. London: Whurr.

Schopler, E. (1995) *Parent Survival Manual*. New York: Plenum Press.

Schopler, E. (1997) 'Implementation of TEACCH philosophy', in Cohen, D. J. and Volkmar, F. R. (eds) *Handbook of Autism and Pervasive Developmental Disorder*. New York: Wiley.

Schopler, E. and Mesibov, G. B. (eds) (1984) *The Effects of Autism on the Family*. New York: Plenum Press.

Trevarthen, C. and Hubley, P. (1978) 'Secondary intersubjectivity', in Lock, A. (ed.) *Action, Gesture and Symbol*. London: Academic Press.

Vetere, A. (1993) 'Using family therapy in services for people with learning disabilities', in Carpenter, J. and Treacher, A. (eds) *Using Family Therapy in the 90's*, Oxford: Blackwell.

Vicary, S. (1985) 'Developments in mothers' construing of their mentally-handicapped one-year-olds', in Beail, N. (ed.) *Repertory Grid Technique and Personal Constructs*. Beckenham: Croom Helm.

White, C. (1997) *Challenging Disabling Practices*. Adelaide: Dulwich.

Winter, D. A. (1992) *Personal Construct Psychology in Clinical Practice*. London: Routledge.

Chapter Seven

Language, Multimedia and Communication for Children with Autism: Searching for the Right Combination

Tomas Tjus and Mikael Heimann

Introduction

Laura, a ten-year-old girl with autism, is looking at the letters in her book. She knows their names very well but when the teacher asks about them Laura does not understand why she is asking. Their shapes look interesting; they look similar to those on the surface of the kitchen table at home. She follows the lines of the letters with her finger. The light that flows from the window is changing depending on what side of the letter she is pointing at. The teacher asks her again but no answer. She waits a while but nothing happens. The teacher gives out a small sigh. The teacher becomes frustrated and starts to feel as if she is hitting a wall. In her mind she thinks: 'Laura knew them several months ago. Why can't she be interested now? What am I doing wrong?'

The teacher talks with Laura's parents. But she gets no support. The parents feel that the teacher doesn't understand their daughter and that the school is unable to bring out her full potential. At home they can feel that Laura is trying to understand what letters mean and what to do with them. Both the parents and the teacher end their talk without having reached any common ground. In silence they blame each other.

We will return to Laura and her situation but we will also describe other children as well when discussing different aspects of learning conditions. Learning new skills can be difficult for any child, but is often especially so for a child with autism. It is a complex situation requiring patience and flexible thinking for both teachers and parents. Still, we often get stuck! This is a situation that creates frustration and a desperate search for good and adequate guidelines specially developed for children with autism. These guidelines are often of an eclectic and pragmatic character prescribing methods that deal primarily with behavioural and symptom related issues. However, there is often a lack of a general theoretical knowledge regarding learning mechanisms, and in particular the role that emotions play is often more or less neglected.

Children with autism are unique with their own special needs but they also share many resources (and problems) with other children with or without disabilities. One such area is their need to feel comfortable and have fun when learning in school, and this chapter will show that factors like enjoyment might also play an important role for children with autism. We will try to demonstrate that an educational strategy that includes enjoyable multimedia material in combination with good teacher support can lead to both better language and communication skills (Heimann *et al.* 1995; Tjus 1998; Tjus *et al.* 1998).

These positive findings were not based on a strategy specifically developed for children with autism. Instead, they were based on a specific theory, the Rare Event Learning (REL) model, which was originally developed by Keith E. Nelson in the USA. This is a dynamic cognitive theory 'under construction' that tries to outline all fundamental components in language learning, not only for children with autism but also children with other disabilities (see Nelson 1991; Nelson *et al.* 1996; Nelson, *et al.* 1997). The main idea behind this model is that in any learning episode a large number of various factors exist at any specific point in time, and that some of them promote development whereas others might hinder the child in his or her learning process. It is extremely rare for enough of these factors to be known or to be blended in a fashion so that optimal learning might occur. This 'tricky mix' of supportive factors is difficult to detect and obtain since each factor is dependent on the rare occasion when all the necessary conditions are in fact at work. A brief overview of some basic assumptions is shown in Figure 7.1.

The specifics of our model and our theory will be described in more detail and in a more concrete fashion as we describe how Laura and other children have been helped or not helped by our approach. However the main content of the REL model can be described here by using the acronym LEARN:

L = launching conditions

These include cognitive factors such as the child's ability to attend to new and challenging structures that are experienced within a verbal dialogue. It has to do with how prepared the child is to learn new things, how able he or she is to capture relevant information and how easily those new structures are encoded into the child's long-term memory. In addition, the teacher may have too high or too low initial expectations of the child's learning potential and thus create a setting in which the child feels uncomfortable and/or unmotivated. It is usually difficult to decide what particular levels or zones of challenge are needed to allow processing and learning by a child at a particular stage of acquisition in speech and text.

E = enhancing conditions

These might include catalysts such as recasts. Here the teacher reformulates the children's utterances (into what may be called 'new syntactic packages'), keeping

CENTRAL COMPONENTS OF THE REL MODEL:
1.   Language delays are produced by multiple factors.
2.   Different factors can operate in individual cases.
3.   Processing capacities influence the interactive dialogue with important partners and contribute to the observed delay.
4.   Children's current knowledge of language structures needs to be challenged by appropriate new input.
5.   Combinations of conditions need to converge, so-called 'tricky mixes', in order for language delayed processes to continue, and these mixes may be very different among individual children.

Figure 7.1 The Rare Event Learning (REL) model

the central meaning but adding something, as in the following illustration:
Child: There is a dog.
Adult: Yes, there is a dog and it is big, isn't it?

Observations by other researchers have demonstrated that the language used by adults when talking to children with various disabilities (e.g. hearing impairment or Down's syndrome) is characterised by a less challenging and more directive speech (Conti-Ramsden 1994; Snow 1995). A similar pattern was found in our own studies (Tjus *et al.* in press): teachers working with children with a lower language level used directives more often and expressed less positive emotions. They also praised the child less often, in spite of the fact that these children increased their ability to focus on and talk about relevant material more than the children with a higher language level! We believe that the main reason why the teachers gave more positive feedback to this latter group was that these children's better language ability meant that they were responding more saliently and were more in tune with the teachers' implicit expectations. The interaction between children and teachers is indeed complex and this brief example illuminates the fact that we, as adults, are influenced by both negative and positive unconscious emotional processes and expectations when working with those children who are furthest behind in terms of achievement. It is our duty to become as aware as possible about our own implicit emotional reactions or expectations.

A = adjustment processes

These include factors such as support from the teacher to the students to overcome frustration and positive reinforcement of the children's self-esteem. This part of the teaching process is particularly important since children with learning disabilities are at high risk of developing associated emotional and adaptive disorders that might contribute to emotional obstacles within the learning process. Poorer self-concepts (general and academic) and lowered expectations have been noted as possible negative outcomes where teacher support is lacking.

R = readiness conditions

These are illustrated by the children's level of functioning and their interest, knowledge and motivation for learning. Thus, assessment of various cognitive abilities is needed before the aims of training are decided. This is extremely important for children with autism since it has been found that (i) communicative language and (ii) cognitive levels are the factors that best predict future progress (Gillberg and Steffenburg 1987). In addition children with disabilities often have problems with self-regulatory strategies that might lead to a lack of checking, planning, and monitoring. They often have difficulties with detecting relevant details and they seldom modify their strategy even after several rounds of negative feedback.

N = network representations

When new language material becomes well rehearsed and well integrated within existing knowledge new and efficient representations are formed. As a consequence, allocation of processing energy becomes more sufficient. For example, a good reader must be able to engage in parallel processing since reading a story requires considerable energy to keep track of all the lexical, syntactic, and discourse information that goes to make up a story. Multimedia materials of the type we have used (described in more detail in Figure 7.2) support parallel processing of more than one structural comparison. It was designed so that each sentence in text corresponded closely to the animated graphic and sentences. Such close correspondence is not typical in instructional sequences with books. Within 20 to 30 seconds all modes of input (animation, text, speech/sign, language) representing the same event can be used to support comparisons.

Hearing children with autism or other disabilities

Child enters text, 'THE DINOSAUR CHASES THE LION'

Multimedia animation, The dinosaur chases the lion

Multimedia voice says, 'The dinosaur chases the lion'

Child comments in voice

Teacher recasts in voice

Deaf children using sign language

Child enters text, 'THE DINOSAUR CHASES THE LION'

Multimedia animation, The dinosaur chases the lion

Multimedia signs, 'The dinosaur chases the lion'

Child comments in sign

Teacher recasts in sign

Figure 7.2 The DeltaMessages multimedia strategy for literacy: examples of interactive sequences (Nelson et al. 1997, p. 299)

The rest of the chapter will describe how these LEARN factors show themselves in a pedagogical setting and how they have influenced our thinking when working with children with autism. But first, a brief interlude that will give an overview of the strategy we have employed and used as an intervention method for children with autism and other children with severe communicative disabilities.

An interactive multimedia based teaching strategy

Our approach is based on two, equally important, factors.
  1. *A highly motivating multimedia environment* In order to achieve this kind of environment we have used specially constructed computer programs. For example, the program we have used most extensively (Nelson and Heimann 1995) makes it possible for a child to construct a sentence in text and then receive immediate multi-channel feedback. Depending on the need of the

individual child, different combinations of language modes might be employed (see Figure 7.2). When creating events (= exploration mode) graphic and speech are presented after the child 'writes a sentence' by clicking component phrases, such as 'The bee hides the carrot.' The test mode, in contrast, starts by showing a graphic video animation to the child. Here the child's task will be to choose, from a set of alternatives, the sentence that most correctly captures the graphic meaning feedback (see Figure 7.3).

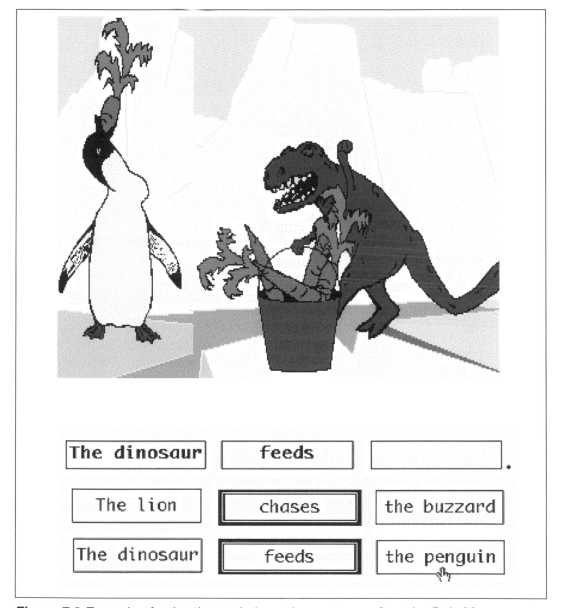

Figure 7.3 Example of animation and alternative sentences from the DeltaMessages in-built-tests

2. *An intense and lively interaction between teacher and child* We know that variations in input might influence both language delay and literacy delay (Nelson 1991; Conti-Ramsden 1994). Among negative components of input are too few stage-relevant challenges, too rapid or too slow communication or too few discourse facilitators of processing (e.g. recasts). Thus, we saw it as centrally important to provide not only an interesting multimedia program, but also interesting conversations. This was achieved via the teachers who were instructed to use a recast strategy when appropriate. We expected that this approach would enhance learning and speed up the pace of language acquisition. In our approach, recasts became a primary enhancer used both in the computer program (built-in multimedia sequences) and through conversational recasting by the teacher.

These two processes, the one going on between the child and the computer and the other between the child and his or her teacher, worked together to create an enjoyable event that promoted learning. Overall two-thirds of all the children participating in our studies to date have made significant gains with our combined multimedia-recasting strategy. The rest of the chapter describes the progress made by some of those children as well as the lack of progress displayed by some others.

Implementing the strategy

Launching

Laura is not making much progress together with her teacher. In fact, the teacher has difficulty just to get her started. Teaching Laura language skills seems almost an impossible task. The teacher uses the strategy that usually works and tries and tries again to make her interested, but to no avail.

The launching aspect deals with both global and detailed processes. Globally it has to do with the overall setting: the teacher needs to create a learning environment tailored to the specific needs of each child. This means thinking about distracters such as noise, light and number of other children in the classroom, and the order of the skills that will be trained during the day. In addition, the desk must be organised in an attractive fashion. These are concrete and often obvious factors that many of the teachers we have met usually are aware of (although the here-and-now situation sometimes makes it difficult to go from what one knows and has planned to what one does).

The detailed launching processes highlight the child's thinking abilities. Is the material to be learnt really within the child's capacity; is he or she ready to 'take in' the relevant information? The delicate task for the teacher or the parent is to find a level that is right on target. If, for instance, we are trying to teach language skills, the child must be able to recognise that there is something to be learnt and attend to the information that is 'out there'. In order to learn new material we need to compare what is already known with the new material presented. We might say that – below awareness – the child's system detects an error signal and tries to minimise this error. Low error means that the system is competent and can make use of the information in an adequate fashion. The goal for the child's system and for the teacher will be to minimise error or to maximise error detection. Laura's teacher needs to experiment with new strategies. This might mean trying something completely new or just gradually modifying the strategy already used until a change in motivation and attention is noted. The teacher needs to avoid a situation that forces Laura to work with too complex material or that overloads the child's system by the way she talks to her. The teacher's sentences might be too long and too complex. Or maybe she just talks too much. All of this might create a situation where the child is unable to distinguish relevant from irrelevant information. And it might also put too much pressure on a weak and fragile memory system.

In short, launching means getting it right from the start – something that is definitely easier said than done. But we must try and try again to find the right entrance to the child's learning system. This means that we need constantly to monitor our own work and our own strategy. We, as well as the children, must learn from previous failure and also recognise and admit our mistakes. We need to use the information gained from what did not work and constantly work towards a better understanding of how learning can be enhanced for just this child.

Enhancement

John is five-years-old, has been diagnosed as autistic and attends a daycare centre where he receives special support by Nils, his personal assistant. Nils clearly understands the importance of creating an enhancing situation for John, to adapt social and cognitive factors to his way of reasoning. After each computer session John wants to compare the length of the printout from the lessons he just completed with his own length. He spreads them out on the floor and lies down beside the paper sheets so that he can make a comparison. If the printout is longer than his length he becomes satisfied and is ready to continue with the next tasks on his curriculum.

To us, the above episode is a rather good example of how a teacher might adapt his way of working to the child's individual symptomatology. Something that is not always done! We have experienced several episodes where the teachers treat the 'method' as more important than the child's actual problems. This creates a situation when the symptom of the child is treated as an unwanted distracter that hinders the teacher from using the most desirable method. This is of course a very rigid way of thinking on the teacher's part but we must remember that it is a trap that most of us can fall into. Our own motivation, interests and personal biases can easily make us so blind that we continue to push for a teaching strategy even though it clearly does not work with the particular child in front of us. What we need to do is constantly to remind ourselves of how important enhancement factors are and also that they differ among children. We need to individualise as much as possible.

One successful enhancement factor is to use the interaction with the child in a more focused way so that learning becomes more probable. This can be done in several ways, but one such procedure is to use recasts as described earlier in this chapter. However, even this procedure can be further enhanced. Usually, recasting is seen as something taking place within a verbal dialogue. The child says something and the teacher or parent uses the child's utterance in order to create an expanded reply, a recast. Within our multimedia framework, the computer also produces recasts as the child receives feedback within several different modalities. A child who has created an interesting event on the screen (e.g. 'The carrot chases the buzzard.') sees the text, hears it spoken and sees it played out as an animated event. Within just a few seconds the child gets to process the same message through three different channels (text, sound and animation). Children using sign language might even receive feedback via a fourth channel: video clips of sign language. In addition, the child often receives real life recasts via the ongoing dialogue with a teacher.

Our multimedia sequences were designed so that the child's limited active processing capacity was directed toward comparisons of new text to already known representations of graphic events or of voice or sign. We expected such intermodal comparisons to facilitate learning and the multimedia strategy gave the child multiple processing opportunities. One such catalyst was the one-to-one nature of the multimedia procedures employed: each sentence in text corresponds closely to the animated graphic and first language (speech or sign) sentences. Recasting creates redundancy in a non-boring fashion; it is not a simple repetition that makes the situation less fun. Instead, recasting via multimedia and the teacher scaffolding the situation increases the likelihood that the child really takes in some new information.

Adjustment

The situation for Laura is uncertain, frustrating and maybe even confusing since she has big problems with connecting her 'two worlds' – the one at home where she is able to show her abilities and the one in school where she hides them.

At this moment the teacher is also in great need of support and the parallel between her and Laura's emotional frustration is obvious from a neutral perspective. Since the teacher is supposed to be the one who can give Laura support and take care of her frustration the situation for Laura at school is unstable. The teacher has started to blame herself, it is her fault and her way of teaching is a failure. Loops of negative emotional feedback might develop. However, these processes are often unconscious and there is also a risk for an escalating conflict between the teacher and the parents, and that prestige will prevent the parents and the teacher from reaching a common understanding. This situation is not uncommon: i.e. that the one who sees the child making progress attributes this gain to his/her competence. Actually, the fact that Laura can read the letters at home is probably a combination of the work in school *and* the emotional adjustment from the parents at home. It is difficult for a teacher to be good enough at all moments for all children. In Laura's case there might be other children in great need of help from the teacher and this might have an impact on the relationship between the teacher and Laura.

The importance of sharing the same perspective could also be further exemplified by our own experience with a specific interactive multimedia strategy. The parents were very often enthusiastic and viewed the project as an opportunity for their children but the teachers did not always share this enthusiasm. Some teachers even felt that they 'needed' to participate in the project because of perceived pressure from the parents, something they rarely told the parents or us directly. Instead, it was something that was revealed slowly as the project continued. If any of the children working with these teachers displayed negative feelings or behaved in a destructive manner, the teachers had difficulty in giving support or showing a positive attitude towards the child. It usually resulted in sustained suffering for both parties.

Mats, a boy with Asperger's syndrome, provides another example of the importance of the emotional climate between the child and the teacher. He was 14-years-old when he participated in our program and he had received his diagnosis just a couple of years earlier. His learning and social problems had previously been labelled by several other less accurate 'diagnostic categories' creating a frustrating and inadequate school situation. It also resulted in conflicts between schools and advocates of various pedagogical methods and his parents. In the end he was enrolled at a school which specialised in working with children with autism where he also met a supportive teacher.

Both Mats' teacher and his parents wanted him to participate in our study and we carried out first assessments before the intervention period started. However, just before the training commenced his teacher was replaced and he had to start working with a new teacher. They ended the computer training right before the summer holidays. Our data revealed that Mats had a moderate increase in reading skills during the months preceding the intervention period (the baseline period: see Figure 7.4) but no increase at all during or after the intervention. Thus, we detected no effect from the training efforts. However, further analysis of Mats' results told us that something peculiar was happening: a considerable gain in reading skills could be seen for the summer holiday. So, what on earth was going on? Should we conclude that Mats did not need the school for learning to read and write, that he was better off staying at home instead?

Further probing into Mats' situation made it clear that saying good-bye to his old teacher (and they liked each other a lot!) created a separation that became too tough for him. He could not accept his new teacher and we also understood that it was tough for her as well. Thus the chance of creating a positive pedagogical climate was minimal. During the summer his mother had decided to put some extra energy into his reading training with very impressive gains as the result. However, when coming back to school for the new semester Mats was placed in a situation where he had to interact with a teacher he did not like, resulting in a very negative

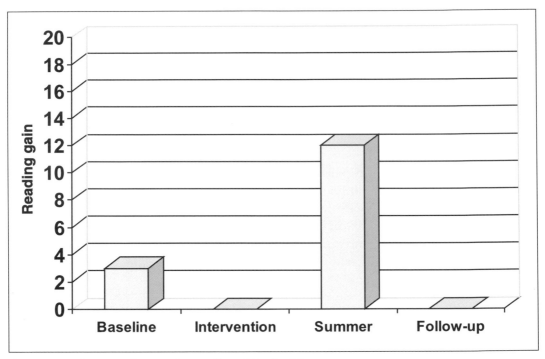

Figure 7.4 Observed gains in reading skills for Mats

outcome. This seems to be a similar situation to that which Laura had experienced. In short, the training with his previous teacher and the emotional adjustment from, and the training with, his mother became an extraordinarily successful combination for Mats.

These examples illustrate the importance of the emotional relationship ('climate') between the child and his or her teacher when defining realistic goals for the training. When deciding which training is needed, the choice must be viewed from different perspectives before it is launched. The daily training for a child with autism can in itself be frustrating and the child's need for emotional support is as huge as is the teacher's and the parents' need. It is clearly unhelpful if an extra burden is placed on the teacher's or the child's shoulders by letting unconscious feelings and expectations become an obstacle.

Readiness and Network

Is the child's cognitive system really ready for a certain type of training and to what extent is this readiness dependent upon previous experiences and already formed networks of mental representations? This question is very difficult to answer when considering the introduction of a new task. Imagine the previous example of Laura knowing the letters by their shape but having problems in generalising her knowledge from her home to the school setting. She is ready and mature enough for the first step in reading training, i.e. letter identification. But is she close to achieving the next step where she is able to detect and solve the reading code? Her problem could be that the underlying meaning of the letters and the use of them will create a chain that is too long – the connections between their shapes and their corresponding sounds have to be put together into words. These words have then to be built together into sentences. At this moment this underlying 'secret message' is too difficult for this girl to decipher. A child without autism would, this far in his or her development, normally have received enough positive rewards through encouragement – from the pleasure and satisfaction shown by both teachers and parents that the child has learnt the letters – to motivate him/herself to explore further, to continue the training. We dare to suggest that this type of emotional reward is often lacking for children with autism. We have observed (by detailed analysis of videotaped lessons) children with autism who seemed to appreciate hearing from their teachers that they were doing well when working with the computer but more often children who did not show any reaction. Thus, timing and emotional adjustment are crucial when hoping that new networks of knowledge will be developed. Especially when traditional positive reinforcements such as enjoyment or praising (e.g. telling a child how good he is) might be ineffective.

In Laura's case her willingness to work with the letters at home might be good enough. If both the parents and the teacher could accept that it is not necessarily a failure that Laura does not show her ability at school the teacher could instead try to see if Laura would like to start phonological training. She could, for instance, try to identify the initial sounds of words e.g. 'm – ummy', 'd – addy'. This would be a wonderful complement to the knowledge she already has and could also be a bridge between her two settings. The traditional view that it is only in the school that children learn school skills, and that the home provides opportunities for learning separate things, is an old fashioned way of thinking. Our view is that all factors that influence children's learning (inside and outside a person) are related and have an impact on the child's skills. This means that if something positive or negative happens in one area – for example in school – it will influence the situation at home. And vice versa, of course.

We offer another example of readiness (interest and motivation) and network (new forms of knowledge) and how difficult it is to estimate when a child is ready to take a new step and the way to make it.

Peter, 13-years-old and actually a very good reader, was asked every Monday by his teacher to write something about what he had done during the past weekend. He was only able to do that in a telegraphic way, e.g. 'bath, daddy, TV' and this went on for several years.

After participating in one of our intervention studies we could detect no progress in reading skills (partly due to ceiling effects) although Peter clearly loved the multimedia environment. However, an important side effect of our strategy was that through his work with our program, by combining and visualising words within a multimedia setting, he became able to write two- and three-word sentences for the first time in his life. That is, Peter now wrote sentences like 'I watched TV.' instead of only 'TV' when asked to write about his activities over the weekend. This was a major step for him (and for the teacher and also for his parents); for the first time he could understand the meaning of combining words in text. By imitating what he had 'written' on the computer he was able to generalise it to the traditional use of pen and paper.

Picking up the pieces

We have tried to show that a specially designed multimedia environment combined with a recasting strategy can have a significant impact on how children with autism learn to read. The intervention has proved effective in promoting both reading and communication skills. A majority of the children with autism that we worked with read better and conversed more after exposure to our strategy. However, even though those results seem to be positive, it must be remembered that the children participating in our studies had all been selected based on prior motivation for language. That is, the parents or the teachers had observed some interest for exploring different aspects of the language. For example, a child might have shown interest in letter identification or in printed text that he or she encountered. We did not work with children displaying no interest in language or communication whatsoever.

Even so, the children we ended up with were a rather heterogeneous group. Some could already read while some had just identified their first letter. Moreover, they also represented a large variation in cognitive abilities (range of IQ: 50–120), giving the teachers a rather difficult task. Here the LEARN framework can help to organise a plan for a better learning environment. The various factors that are included (Launching, Enhancement, Adjustment, Readiness and Network) do overlap with one another but, at the same time, the framework provides the teacher with a scheme that helps to structure thinking about the way in which teaching and learning may proceed in the immediate future. It might also hopefully function as a catalyst for further discussions or reflections upon the way the daily curriculum is organised.

Finding the tricky mix of conditions needed to support the learning of any child with autism is likely to require more ingenuity and wider exploration of combinations of conditions than is required by most other teachers. But the payoffs of active exploration of conditions can be very high, as is evident by the cases used to illustrate this chapter as well as by observations made by others. For example, a child with autism has been observed to acquire the word 'sidewalk' in just two quick trials, with clear encouragement in the real-world context of examining chalk writing on a sidewalk (Koegel & Koegel 1995). It is our belief that, under new mixes of conditions where challenges and human support are finely attuned to the individual learner, even children with autism will show learning rates that match those of learners with no disabilities (Nelson, *et al.* 1997).

The learning capacity of children and people with autism still remains a puzzle to a large degree. We usually do not know when certain skills will be impossible to learn despite extensive learning opportunities, yet at the same time other skills will reach quite surprisingly high levels. What exactly are the mixes of conditions that prove to be ineffectual despite teachers' most vigorous efforts, as opposed to very powerful, effective mixes based on the LEARN framework? For some children with autism it has proved feasible to use sign language which has revealed excellent learning capacities and communicative progress, in contrast to objectively meagre prior progress in spoken language across many years of trying various ways of mixing social and language challenges (e.g. Bonvillian *et al.* 1981).

Many theorists claim that working memory processes are central in learning new communicative structures (e.g. Gathercole and Baddeley 1993). The children's working memory abilities were not evaluated in our studies but it might be speculated that – within our multimedia framework – increasing the relevant information and decreasing the irrelevant information facilitated these processes. Multimedia and recasts specifically help memory processes by creating a situation allowing rich connections between representations of the same meaning in different modes but avoiding excessive processing demands.

To sum it up, clear gains in literacy skills have been found for children with autism when training with our multimedia computer program in combination with a specific teacher strategy. But why is this 'package' so attractive for these children? One explanation may be that they have problems that resemble those shown by children with Attention Deficit and Hyperactivity Disorder (ADHD) (Barkley *et al.* 1992; Hughes, *et al.* 1994) like planning and flexible adaptation to new instructions and changed routines. The opportunity to explore the lessons freely and create the same sentence again and again with immediate feedback makes them channel into creative processing some of the repetitive and perseverative behaviours that can be a huge problem in any regular school setting. The immediate feedback may also help them to feel that they have taken control of the learning situation and that the rules for social interaction, one of the core problems in autism (Frith 1989; Wing 1989), become more understandable when working with the computer.

We have also speculated that the triad of child, teacher and attractive computer material might create a favourable situation for joint attention and related verbal exposure. In infancy normally developing children use the head and eye movements of both the infant and the mother as referential cues towards a joint attention of objects and this is strongly related to the mother's vocalisation; probably one of the major conceptual pathfinders to verbal acquisition (Locke 1995). For children with autism this mechanism might be very difficult to obtain in ordinary interaction since, for them, perceiving others' intentions and referential communication are core problems.

Acknowledgements

This joint paper owes its result to grants from the Swedish Council of Social Research, Stockholm, to Mikael Heimann (grant 92-0173) and Erland Hjelmquist (grant 95-0915); from Queen Silvia's Jubilee Fund for Research on Children and Handicaps to Tomas Tjus; and from the Swedish Transport & Communications Research Board (grant 1999-0181) to Mikael Heimann. We also wish to thank all the participating children and their families as well as their teachers.

References

Barkley, R. A., Grodzinsky, G. and DuPaul, G. J. (1992) 'Frontal lobe functions in attention deficit disorder with and without hyperactivity: a review and research report', *Journal of Abnormal Child Psychology* 2, 163–88.

Bonvillian, J. D., Nelson, K. E. and Rhyne, J. M. (1981). 'Sign language and autism', *Journal of Autism and Developmental Disorders,* **11**, 125–137.

Conti-Ramsden, G. (1994) 'Language interaction with atypical language learners', in Gallaway, C. and Richards, B. (eds) *Input and Interaction in Language Interaction.* London: Cambridge University Press.

Frith, U. (1989) *Autism: Explaining the Enigma.* Oxford: Basil Blackwell.

Gathercole, S. E. and Baddeley, A. D. (1993) *Working Memory and Language.* Hillsdale, NJ: Erlbaum.

Gillberg, C. and Steffenburg, S. (1987) 'Outcome and prognostic factors in infantile autism and similar conditions. A population based study of 46 cases followed through puberty', *Journal of Autism and Developmental Disorders* **17**, 271–85.

Heimann, M., Nelson, K. E., Gillberg, C. and Tjus, T. (1995) 'Increasing reading and communication skills in children with autism through an interactive multimedia program', *Journal of Autism and Developmental Disorders* **25**, 459–80.

Hughes, C., Russell, J. and Robbins, T. W. (1994) 'Evidence for executive dysfunctions in autism', *Neuropsychologia* **4**, 477–92.

Koegel, L. K. and Koegel, R. L. (1995) 'Motivating communication in children with autism', in Schopler, E. and Mesibov, G. B. (eds) *Learning and Cognition in Autism.* New York: Plenum Press.

Locke, J. L. (1995) 'Development of capacity for spoken language', in Fletcher, P. and MacWhinney, B. (eds) *The Handbook of Child Language.* Oxford: Blackwell Publishers.

Nelson, K. E. (1991) 'On differentiated language learning models and differentiated interventions', in Krasnegor, N., Rumbaugh, D. and Schiefelbusch, R. (eds.) *Language Acquisition: Biological and Behavioral Determinants.* Hillsdale, NJ: Erlbaum.

Nelson, K. E., Camarata, S. M., Welsh, J., Butkovsky, L. and Camarata, M. (1996) 'Effects of imitative and conversational recasting treatment on the acquisition of grammar in children with specific language impairment and younger language-normal children', *Journal of Speech and Hearing Research* **39**, 850–59.

Nelson, K. E. and Heimann, M. (1995) *DeltaMessages, Computer Software Program*. Warriors Mark, PA: Super Impact Images and Göteborg, Sweden: Topic Data-och Språkbehandling Hb.

Nelson, K. E., Heimann, M. and Tjus, T. (1997), 'Theoretical and applied insights from multimedia facilitation of communication skills in children with autism, deaf children, and children with other disabilities', in Adamson, L. B. and Romski, M. A. (eds) *Communication and Language Acquisition: Discoveries from Atypical Development*. Baltimore, MD: Paul Brookes Publishers.

Snow, C. E. (1995) 'Issues in the study of input: Finetuning, universality, individual and developmental differences, and necessary causes', in Fletcher, P. and MacWhinney, B. (eds) *The Handbook of Child Language*. Oxford: Blackwell Publishers.

Tjus, T. (1998) *Language and Literacy Acquisition in Children with Developmental and Learning Disabilities*. Doctoral Dissertation. Göteborg University, Sweden.

Tjus, T., Heimann, M. and Nelson, K. E. (1998) 'Gains in literacy through the use of a specially developed multimedia computer strategy: Positive findings from 13 children with autism', *Autism: The International Journal of Research and Practice* **2**(2), 139–156.

Tjus, T., Heimann, M., and Nelson, K. E. (in press) 'Interaction patterns between children and their teachers when using a specific multimedia and communication strategy: Observations from children with autism and mixed handicaps'. Submitted manuscript.

Wing, L. (1989) 'The diagnosis of autism', in Gillberg, C. (ed.) *Diagnosis and Treatment of Autism*. New York: Plenum Press.

Chapter Eight

Using Humour to enable Flexibility and Social Empathy in Children with Asperger's Syndrome: Some Practical Strategies

Elizabeth Newson

Introduction

Able autistic (Asperger) children are the most likely to attend mainstream schools, and the least likely to be offered teaching that directly addresses the impairments of their condition; yet their deficits are of the same nature as those of 'ordinary' autistic children, albeit usually operating to a milder degree. This chapter is about specific strategies which have proved helpful to such children in weekly two-hour out-of-school sessions; they could be still more effectively offered by support staff within the integrating school, and many would be entirely appropriate for parents to use at home. Most of our research, diagnostic and interventional work at Nottingham in the field of autism has focused on the more usual range of autistic children: those who have intellectual impairments as well as the essential diagnostic criteria. However, we have also had a special interest in children in the normal and above-average range of intelligence, and we have held three Department of Health grants to look at this group specifically. These various contacts, as well as long-term clinical experience, made it abundantly clear that Asperger children do meet the same defining criteria as the less able children, and that the only divergences between the ways in which the criteria are shown in the more able and the less able are entirely accounted for by the effect of better intellectual function, which enables good verbal ability in terms of grammar and syntax. In fact, the differences between less able autistic children and the more able or Asperger children can be seen as no greater than those we expect to find between bright and intellectually disabled children in the areas of deafness, blindness or cerebral palsy. Thus the language problems of Asperger children are in terms of a semantic-pragmatic disorder which impedes their *social use* of language, even though their grammar and vocabulary may be almost too perfect (pedantic) for natural conversation. Poor social timing governs both verbal and body language, and the pragmatics are almost all affected; while the semantic problem is mainly about understanding the *personal* meanings or intentions of others. Social impairment is seen in more able, as in less able, children as impaired social empathy. In Asperger children this is shown in more complex contexts, reflecting the different expectations we have of a more able child; for instance, bringing a conversation to an abrupt halt by walking away; not answering, or making personal and derogatory remarks in public in a loud voice; or – my favourite example – the adolescent who failed to check out what a non-autistic person would know was a mis-hearing, and bought his mother clothes when all she had asked for was cloves. Inflexibility of thought processes appears in obsessional, repetitive and stereotypic behaviour (including verbal behaviour), extreme literality (difficulty in playing with words – puns, metaphors, sarcasm, jokes, teasing etc.), and insistence on sameness; there is limited symbolic play (e.g. *arrangements* of models rather than open-ended stories in action) and difficulty with role-play.

All the activities described in this chapter have been tried out with several children in a range of clinical and naturalistic settings and found effective – not in curing autism, of course, but in helping relatively bright children and adolescents with Asperger's syndrome to tune in a little better to the way in which ordinary people think and behave – to gain a degree of social empathy, in fact, and to improve their flexibility of thinking. Obviously we have only been able to do this by managing to tune in to *them*, using the flexibility and social empathy that we are fortunate enough to possess.

In practice, these two aims work together to help the child improve his interactional experience with others; this is one reason why I have preferred the term 'social empathy' to 'theory of mind', feeling that notions of theory of mind give a cognitive emphasis which I do not want. Clearly there are cognitive implications in rigidity of thought processes; but I suspect that in remediative terms we quickly reach a ceiling to our endeavours if we are unable to access the social difficulties, which in any case can seldom in practice be separated from the actual operation of cognitive behaviour. In discussing these strategies, then, I acknowledge our special debts to a number of children who have, both bemusedly and amusedly, given us their cooperation and friendship; for convenience, I shall call them James, Martin, William, Ben, Stephen, Luke, Richard, Paul and David. I should perhaps add that I also wear a parental hat, with a son in this same group, and that this has certainly helped me in tuning in to the finer details of the syndrome and to a pragmatic approach (in two senses) to intervention.

The activities
Exploring metaphor

Verbal metaphor
Parents of verbal autistic children often try, with difficulty, to avoid using metaphor in their language because it makes the child so anxious. Common phrases such as 'I could eat a horse', 'He's a bit under the weather' or 'Pick your feet up, get cracking', interpreted literally, can at best confuse, at worst frighten the child. I was

horrified to be accused by my son in adolescence: 'You used to threaten that I'd die'; this turned out to refer to 'Come on, get your jersey on, you'll catch your death!', a quote from my own grandmother which did not perturb his younger sisters in any way. Richard uses metaphor with great ease now, probably as a result of years of listening with one ear as his sisters were read to; his own preference was for information books, which are not the best source of metaphor, though he came to like science fiction and poetry eventually. Literal interpretation in children with autism can extend to visual misinterpretation: for instance, I know several who have screamed with terror on 'mislaying' their own feet in murky seawater, have been reassured by lifting them to see that they were still there, and then screamed again on losing them once more.

We did not feel very hopeful about the efficacy of deliberately teaching a repertoire of metaphors to children, but it was at least a start. James, with whom we began at eight years, clearly thought we were a little crazy, and could hardly believe it when we told him that lots of people used and understood (in a different way from him!) phrases like 'bend over backwards', 'draw a blank' and 'on top of the world'. Like many Asperger children, he had always been amused by what he perceived as bizarre; our interest in teaching metaphor clearly came in that category, so he was happy to have a giggle or two at our expense. We used a series of booklets for ordinary children by Len Collis (now out of print) called *Things We Say: a book that helps you to understand what people mean*; there are others similar, but these we thought the clearest, with explanations in simple language and illustrations that were straightforwardly amusing (some illustrations pose their own problems of visual metaphor for autistic children, we find!).

James happily learned about 50 metaphors by heart, and then began to use them in real conversation situations: the first time in a 'what if' exchange about 'suppose there were burglars next door', with a triumphant 'We could dash in and *catch them red-handed* !' At the end of the nine months' attachment, James's new flexibility with words was helping his tolerance of difference: on one occasion I handed him a drink in a mug which I immediately realised from his face he didn't like; but instead of handing it back (or shouting as he might have done two years previously), he took a drink from it, saying thoughtfully 'You can't judge a drink by its mug - *that's* like "You can't judge a book by its cover".'

Martin at six years was really amused by the whole exercise, and accepted it with alacrity as his main project for the year. During my initial explanation, he repeated each example under his breath, and started to put the phrases into his own favourite kind of structure: 'It rained on Thursday 26th September, so I could say "It's raining cats and dogs!".' I agreed enthusiastically: 'Right, you're getting the hang of it!' – and at once realised that I had inadvertently piled on yet another metaphor which needed explanation. A few minutes later, Martin offered 'My Dad's doing nightwork this month. He's getting the hang of doing nightwork this month!' with a smile all over his face. Martin was later to develop additional layers to the exercise by not only deciding what the metaphor *didn't* mean in literal terms, but also finding some other, often punning version that it also *didn't* mean: ' "Too big for your boots" doesn't mean you're too big to get into Boots (the chemist) in Nottingham!' Flexibility began to develop its own impetus.

Visual correspondences

When we think about correspondences in Baudelaire's sense – the notion that one can conceptualise the smell of a day, the colour of a piece of music, the sound of an abstract shape and so on – we can see that these too are essentially metaphors, and might be helpful as ideas for a child with rigid thought processes. For children who are relatively chatty, or can be induced to be so on certain occasions, a game or running conversation based on these notions might be enough; though we find it helpful to perpetuate what we do in a project book, to encourage the child to look through it outside sessions, and perhaps to talk about its contents to his family or teacher. (Of course, metaphor can itself become somewhat obsessional – but at least one is choosing a constructive preoccupation, which was a consolation for Martin's parents!) As the content is far more important than the academic output in this kind of project, and it is vital that the child should enjoy the sessions, who actually does any 'boring bits' in producing the book is negotiable, and honour can be well satisfied so long as the child contributes ideas, and looks at the book afterwards.

When we started using correspondences with James at the age of eight, he needed more structure than 'chatting', so we decided to invite him to 'paint his emotions', later going on to painting sounds. Both involved abstract use of colours and strokes, and this was an added bonus: James had tended to value only photographic realism in drawing, and was constantly dissatisfied with his usual efforts. The need to paint emotions released him from such inflexible judgements, and also gave a focus for a kind of commentary from the adult: 'that looks like a *really* angry mood, now show me how it is when you just begin to feel a little bit better'. James much enjoyed these painting sessions, but again found it a very extraordinary thing to do: his comment 'I bet I'm the first person who's ever painted emotions' showed how out of touch he was with the ideas which have enabled abstract art and which other children easily assimilate. None the less, James was capable of developing such ideas when he was directly encouraged to do so. Another child (in our research sample) had been helped to control his outbursts by drawing them as colour-insertions on a grid – one of the very few examples of metaphor work emerging from that research.

Puns and other plays on words

Jokes and riddles

As we can see from James's and Martin's pleasure in our 'bizarre' behaviour, Asperger children can have a sense of humour; on the whole, though, it tends to be of the 'banana-skin' variety. With verbal children it seems important deliberately to cultivate a verbal sense of humour, of which the simplest form is probably the pun; and this is a good way to begin. Some children get anxious about words that have two meanings (or objects that have two names, another ambiguity), so finding the humour in this rather than avoiding puns can defuse the anxiety.

There are many collections of jokes on the market, often of the '1000 Worst Jokes' variety which are inevitably a good source of puns; some need expurgation, and it is safest to go for those published by Penguin in the Puffin Books series, of which there are several in print. The Ahlbergs' *The Old Joke Book,* with a strong visual element, is another winner. It is important not to assume the child understands the joke just because he laughs; like the rest of us, autistic children can laugh politely when they don't actually 'get it' – though they probably do so because they have been set on course for a series of laughter-points, almost ritual fashion.

It is worth persisting with the tedious business of working through the reason why the joke is funny, because generalisation does in the end take place with these more able children, and a new era of social possibilities may result. Richard, who had a hard time from other children in his mainstream comprehensive school, did find himself admired and valued for a long cartoon saga in his rough notebook, full of jokes at the expense of school staff; though the tolerance of the staff was tested – and won, following discussion with the Head!

Riddles usually have a joke embedded in them in children's publications. The 'Knock, knock'/'Who's there?' ones depend on a punning element, involve a structured verbal dialogue, and may eventually be made up by the child, perhaps with help. Martin and I were responsible for this one:

Knock knock
Who's there?
William
William who?
Will ya marry me, darling?

Seeing the joke of the riddle's answer involves a swift change of perspective (an abstract and complex form of 'shift of attention' in Courchesne's term),which is precisely what autistic children find difficult but which the brighter children can achieve with a lot of practice. Consider the verbal shifts involved in these two 'waiter, waiter' jokes (from *The Old Joke Book*):

Waiter, waiter, is there soup on the menu?
No, Madam - I wiped it off!

Waiter, waiter, this egg is bad!
Don't blame us, sir, we only laid the table.

Both rigidity of thought process and lack of social empathy are directly addressed by jokes like these, because the cognitive transformation is accompanied by a change of perspective from the customer's point of view to the waiter's. One would find it hard to devise better material for the remediative purpose we have in mind.

Producing a book of riddles and jokes, some borrowed or collected from others but just a few made up, can be very rewarding; word processors and copiers can be brought into action to make the 'book' more authentic. We have sometimes worked with one child to produce a magazine to which the other children attending the Unit contribute; obviously this could more easily be done in a school, where the children are present together, and where teachers could also suggest their favourite jokes, involving additional social contacts.

Other humour

Having begun with jokes and riddles, partly because they come in conveniently short bursts for the child to cope with in the early stages, it then becomes possible to go on to more sustained humour. Comics of the *Dandy* and *Beano* type are useful; more sophisticated and much more sustained are the books of Raymond Briggs, which use the punchy comic-strip format to give a strong visual crutch to verbal understanding. Particularly recommended is *Fungus the Bogeyman*, which appeals to the very normal jokey attraction of all things yukky, and thus helps to bring the autistic child into the humorous traditions of his peers. James slept with *Fungus the Bogeyman* under his pillow for about three years, giving himself a quick giggle first thing in the morning and last thing at night.

This book has a quite sophisticated vocabulary and is not afraid of the long, complex and sometimes abstruse words which intellectually able autistic children often very much enjoy:

> Bogeyboots are watertight and are filled with a mixture of dirty water and grume* or gleet* after being put on.
> *grume: a fluid of thick viscous consistence *gleet: a purulent or morbid discharge

One particular strength is its irony, which opens up a new dimension of humour for the child; for instance, Fungus muses: 'I'm a very lucky Bogey really... nice damp dump... never dries out... always full of flies'; and an information slot about Bogey television explains that 'Programmes are on the usual bogey interests – Filth and Muck, or Gloom, Despondency and Dark, but occasionally, late at night, when the Bogey babies are safely in bed, horror films are shown of sunlight, flowers, cornfields and hot dry beaches with Drycleaners laughing gaily and playing loud music.' James in adolescence has a strong capacity for irony in his own conversation, as does Richard. Since this trait is quite unusual for Asperger adults, it seems likely that a copious diet of *Fungus* and similar books has had something to do with this important skill, which makes both of them much better company.

A further reason why *Fungus* has been so popular for bright autistic children is probably that much of it is in the form of a spoof information book. Where ordinary children may be helped by a storyline to make the informational bits more palatable, for autistic children it is usually the other way round: information is what they like best, and stories about people need too much social empathy to be very rewarding. Once they have understood and accepted that the information here *is itself a joke* (and they may need a year or two of preparation via ordinary jokes and metaphor), this is a format which they are very ready to enjoy. *Fungus* is one of the most sustained and rich versions of the genre, but there are other spoof information books available, three of the best and simplest being the Ahlbergs' *The Worm Book*, Malcolm Bird's *The Witch's Handbook* and Alan Snow's *How Dogs Really Work*. An adult example, of course, is Douglas Adams' *The Hitch-Hiker's Guide to the Galaxy*, to which Richard graduated with pleasure after a helpful period of enjoying science fiction.

'Let's suppose that...'

For children whose depleted imaginative and symbolic play is very obvious evidence of their inflexible thinking, and whose pretend play has been largely a matter of arranging little cars, trains and landscape material rather than inventing adventures with them, 'just imagine' is not a fruitful suggestion. However, there is no need to give up on the idea of 'pretending'; rather, the need is to find a structure which will make the child feel safe enough to venture out into fantasy. This can be done through the media of conversation, sagas, drawing, puppet sketches and even role-play.

The other-way-round world

This idea developed out of the kind of conversation which James, Martin, Richard and Ben all find so rewarding: where you take a basically cognitive notion and explore it in 'What if?' terms. It started by James, as usual, going on about his preoccupation of the moment, which happened to be solar systems. Since the adults on holiday with him were becoming healthily bored with the subject, while the children were ignoring him, one of us started to fantasise about another world that hadn't been discovered yet, where everything was 'the other way round': so, cats barked and dogs mewed, fish caught humans on the end of a line with a Mars bar for bait, you went to the doctor saying 'Doctor, doctor, please make me ill' (or alternatively, the doctor said to the patient 'Thank goodness you've come, I've got a dreadful stomach-ache') – and so on, *ad infinitum*. Other adults became amused and interested on this first occasion, and James was swept along by the impetus and started contributing his own ideas. The secret of this work is both that the imaginative element is given a logical cognitive framework (e.g. if it is an other-way-round world, then such-and-such logically follows), and that the child is caught up in the humour of it. On this occasion the idea became a sort of saga or family joke for the group on holiday; when we came to the last day and held our usual informal concert party, the high spot was a puppet play in which James enacted with his helper the arrival of a boy from Earth on this strange planet, and his conversations with the natives.

Martin at ten years used *The Worm Book* as inspiration for a long project entitled 'What if worms ruled the world?' As well as rules for people and school curricula, he invented TV programmes and game shows, and other activities that took the worms' point of view. Similar work can be done by parents, often involving siblings without a disability: our own family had an imaginary country which was planned in great detail entirely on long car journeys. This may need some careful supervision to prevent any obsessional features becoming too overpowering for the siblings to enjoy the activity. Richard, like many Asperger people, was preoccupied with justice at the time, and beginning to read rather single-tracked political books; he insisted on a democratic constitution while his sister liked the idea of a benevolent autocracy. Our country ended up being ruled by two prime ministers with different areas of responsibility.

'What if things were different...'

The simple question of 'What if...?' can be used effectively for project work or just conversation, without the more worked-out and extended idea of a world or country. The child is simply asked to consider consequences, not in world terms but of one *condition* being different from the familiar one. What if we walked on our hands instead of our feet – what would be the consequences for the furniture? – for clothes? – and so on. What if we could only breathe in water? Again, humour is the oil that lubricates the child's growing flexibility of thought.

Living dangerously, breaking conventions

Ben at eight years was a child whose life was lived entirely by rules. He draws in amazing perspective, but almost his only subjects then were trains and Volkswagen 'Beetles', both of which he could draw from any angle or, in the case of trains, from changing angles. He has his own impressive train layout and a great collection of trains; unfortunately, some of these were out of use because Ben would only run a train which was painted in current British Rail livery, and if British Rail decided to change a livery, another of Ben's trains was put away forever. Similarly, Ben would scream if by accident he came upon a steam train which was no longer in service, perhaps kept on show in a station: 'It doesn't exist!' he would yell in real distress, and his parents learned to avoid such encounters.

Ben collects lots of informational brochures and catalogues on Beetles, and is interested in the various ways they can be customised. This was our cue, because Ben was inclined to be rigid about the choices that were possible, as set out in the customisation brochures. We started by getting Ben to draw an imaginary outing with his therapist; obviously they were to go in a Beetle, but what else could be added into the picture? An increasingly full landscape in which a picnic was taking place was already breaking Ben's rules for a satisfactory picture; but his therapist then decided she wanted Ben to customise the car for her. At first he was inclined to say (rather like any car salesman), 'You can only have that kind of exhaust with this kind of wheeldisc' or 'That colour only comes with this type of graphics'; but he found, to his amazement and amusement, that this customer was insistent on having a Beetle such as had never been seen anywhere, though she was willing to take his advice if he could come up with entirely new features. Because Ben liked his therapist, despite considering her a little mad, he accepted her whims – even when she asked for traffic indicators that were totally out of production. Caroline's year with Ben was largely aimed at helping him to throw aside some of the many conventions which caged his way of thinking; his literality was also challenged by work with metaphor, and Ben accepted this, although previously he had been very anxious when his parents used metaphor, and would plead 'Don't say it again!' On the principle of flooding, repeated metaphor can be less agitating than occasional use. Ben was the major contributor, 18 months later, to Tim Webb's multi-award-winning animated film, *A is for Autism*, which was a very real collaboration between Tim and a group of adults and children with Asperger's syndrome.

What's silly about...?

The ability to see what is silly or funny about a story or picture demands an awareness of the contrasting but absent non-silly alternative. Abstract thought is involved, and so we are not surprised to find such items in the Stanford Binet intelligence test (Terman and Merrill 1960); but from the Asperger point of view the difficult requirement is *flexible* thought. Therapists can produce their own drawn, written or spoken materials; the best ready-made examples I know of are the 'What's Wrong Cards' from Learning Deveopment Aids (Duke St., Wisbech, Cambs. PE13 2AE). There are two sets of about 60 picture cards, one in cartoon form, the other photographic; it is a moot point which are more difficult. They show such scenes as a man with an open umbrella, from inside which the rain is dripping into a pool around his feet; an armchair with human arms; a boy kicking a cauliflower; a woman putting a tray of uncooked cakes into a washing machine; and so on. These give very good linguistic practice in explaining; but some children also have some difficulty scanning to see what is wrong in the first place, though they may find it very funny when they do see it. Stephen at 11 years showed most of his sense of humour in 'what's silly', though he still found puns and metaphor totally obscure.

On camera: make a speech, grab a persona

Over the years we have frequently used video with children we are working with, in social skills groups, individual projects and on 'independence holidays'. Some of the most useful ideas have come out of the holiday situations, when the children are very much in a mood to enjoy themselves and seem especially relaxed. Many of the valuable 'happenings' we have filmed have been done on the spur of the moment, without thought or preparation by anyone. For instance, a child dressing up as a bride in net curtains triggered an impromptu wedding, for which one Asperger child sang a hymn, another collected the signatures of witnesses, while a third, Paul, gave a short but serious sermon on love and marriage (he had already lectured us at length on the habits of caterpillars and butterflies, his preoccupying topic, so he needed only a little adaptation!).

That same evening, at supper, I invited Paul to say grace, which he did with alacrity, returning to his 'vicar' role. I pushed my luck, asking each of the seven children to do something I thought they could manage, and ending with 'James, get up and make a speech', which I wasn't at all sure he could or would do. James was caught up in the general excitement, stood up on his chair, and delivered an extraordinary harangue for ten minutes on the dangers of creatures from outer space; unsmiling and in full flood, he was able to answer questions from the floor in this serious role, and eventually had to be gently brought to a close. This experience, however, certainly gave him enormous confidence (aged ten); the fact that it had been filmed by our roving video-person somehow proved to him that he could do such things, and was the beginning of an enthusiasm for role play which he took with him into comprehensive school, to the drama staff's astonishment.

Interestingly, videoing this unprepared incident had another spin-off for James; after watching the tape and enjoying the praise for his performance, he asked me privately 'Do I always rock like that?' Like so many Asperger people, James did tend to rock on his feet when carried away by enthusiasm, and I told him truthfully 'Not always, but quite often'. His response was 'I don't like it, it looks silly.' I suggested 'You could work on that next term if you like', and he gladly accepted. Clearly it is helpful if a child is self-motivated by his own perception of what needs help, and video can achieve this.

Stephen has made two videos, one with himself as a celebrity on a Wogan-type interview, another showing the viewers around his new house and garden; both have stimulated sustained language as well as empathy for the camera-person. Richard at ten years was helped to join his younger sisters 'playing schools' by being allocated the role of visiting lecturer, in which he gave the assembled dolls the benefit of his considerable knowledge of certain preoccupying topics; for the pleasure of doing this, he was prepared to go along with the pretend world of the dolls, which he had regarded as 'silly'. This role was later adapted more flexibly into genuinely helping his sisters with their homework (which required social empathy for their needs), and sowed the seeds for his adult profession as a successful lecturer and consultant in medical statistics.

'Advanced' social empathy

As the children grew through adolescence, we have needed to look for more complex and taxing ways of refining their social empathy since they were now capable of this. Many of the group games suggested in drama workshop handbooks, especially the 'non-competitive' games, are suitable for enhancing empathy and can often be adapted for one-to-one work. It is worth looking at the various boxed games in toyshops with social empathy in mind; many of them call for the participant to make a guess at what his opponent is thinking (or is seeing in his or her 'hand'), and such games can present a real challenge to otherwise very able young people. 'Happy Families' and other such card games are good examples, but there are many more novel games which have attractive and amusing features in the way they are presented and therefore keep motivation high through a difficult task: an example is 'Guess Who?' (M and B Games), which involves a board with lots of pop-up faces, has a good logical basis to support the able autistic child, but also demands a degree of empathy which creates a real stumbling block.

The most sophisticated game we have used, and with particular success, has been the adult game of 'Scruples' (Milton Bradley). I first realised the problems, and therefore the potential, of this game when James, on holiday with my family, attempted to play it with us. The game involves the participants considering a series of social or ethical dilemmas (e.g. 'You lose an expensive gold watch and are reimbursed by your insurance company. Shortly afterwards you find the watch – do you return the money?'), and then predicting what other participants would say if faced with such a dilemma (in three categories - YES, NO or IT DEPENDS). Scoring can be by correct prediction, but there is room for bluffing, and you may then challenge the other participant by arguing why you believe your prediction is correct, while she defends by argument her own position; the affair is then settled by general vote.

James had great difficulty, as one might expect, with the grey area of 'IT DEPENDS', and never used this to start with, which certainly put him at a disadvantage. This alone would have made the game an attractive one on which to base the following year's programme; but the need to predict other people's views gave still richer promise. On this first occasion James was aghast when I answered 'It depends' to the dilemma of whether I would appear naked on the centrefold of a magazine, and firmly argued that my answer *must* be 'No' because I was 'too old and too fat'. However, he was prepared to consider my argument that it depended on the amount of money offered and (crucially) whether my face would be shown.

The game was eventually adapted to one-to-one play by using 'stand-ins' for other people James knew, and in various forms the structure underpinned a whole year's work which paid off enormously in James's increasing interest in 'how people think and feel' and in personal relationships generally. Some of the benefits were unforeseen. For instance, after a few weeks James pointed out that some of these printed dilemmas (e.g. 'Your mate has been unfaithful – do you leave him or her?') had little relevance to an adolescent boy like himself, so it was suggested to him that he might like to produce an entirely new set of dilemmas which *were* relevant to him. This exercise, which he much enjoyed, was very valuable in itself: both because it sharpened his own awareness of dilemmas generally, and his in particular, and because it offered the therapist a window on these which James usually kept firmly shut. More important still, however, was that his new list of dilemmas formed the basis for a series of counselling opportunities over the rest of the year: once James had been facilitated by the game's structure to admit to his dilemmas, there no longer seemed an insuperable barrier to putting them on the agenda for much more open discussion.

Overview and evaluation

The activities that I have discussed have not been evaluated in formal ways; we are still at the stage of working on the problems that present by whatever means we can. Given that we started by taking account of the underlying deficits of autism in quite direct ways, we would expect some measure of success. Perhaps the first measure is in simple terms of survival in mainstream: all the children named except Paul, with whom we have only had brief holiday contact, have coped in mainstream school, and those old enough to take public examinations have been successful. The oldest, whose initial presentation in terms of stereotypes and obsessional behaviour was at the 'severe' extreme of our Asperger research sample, is now also the most successful in terms of academic and job achievement following sustained interventions of these kinds; and James so far has done extremely well academically, despite a severity of condition that necessitated a specialist school for his first three years; younger children seem very much on a similar course.

However, we are aware that this has been a small group of children who were fortunate enough to live close to a university research group specialising in pervasive developmental disorders, which also had the luxury of including this kind of contact as part of the curriculum for developmental psychology postgraduates. Much more beneficial would be to introduce such activities into the remedial programme offered within the mainstream schools where most Asperger children should be receiving support that allows for one-to-one contact periods.

Most of what has been described has in fact taken place on a one-to-one basis, and this has often seemed crucial in making it possible to monitor closely the child's appreciation of humour, with a rapid response to any difficulty. It must be evident that most of the time we have been dependent on the child's goodwill, which has itself been earned through his perception of the enjoyable possibilities of humour. Thus what we have been asking of the child has never really seemed like 'learning asocially'; and in fact there have been many examples of the child tolerating the learning because he found our aims and behaviour amusing. The social relationship, *facilitated* by humour, has been an essential thread in the 'therapeutic strand' that Christie (1986) identifies as a necessity for the successful education of a child with autism.

Nonetheless, there have been times when a small group, usually including other children with autism and their support workers, has given an impetus of excitement not otherwise available, and it has been clear that children have been carried along on a wave of shared enthusiasm. James's rousing speech at the supper-table would have been unlikely in one-to-one; so would Paul's sustained role-play as vicar, without a wedding and a respectful audience. The 'concert-party' performances on the last day of our 'independence holidays' often seemed the result of what we came to call 'excitement therapy'; with only one hour for each child and helper to plan their contribution, being swept along could be crucial to success. When David, an autistic child with moderate learning difficulties, animatedly performed with his helper a slapstick dialogue between two furry animal glove puppets, it was not until the following day that we learned from his parents, as they watched the video, that 'David *never* touches fur. How did you get him to do that?' We had no answer; all we had done was to say 'Quick, quick David – we're on!'

The mainstream school with keyworker support, so necessary (if we take the long-term view) in ensuring usable qualifications for job prospects in later life for Asperger people, would seem ideally placed to provide the enhanced curriculum the child requires. However, it does need flexibility and social empathy, as well as a sense of humour, from those who plan the Asperger child's support, and a realisation that these qualities are wholly appropriate ingredients for a broad, balanced *and relevant* education. Is that too much to ask?

References

Adams, D. (1979) *The Hitch-Hiker's Guide to the Galaxy*. London: Pan Books.

Ahlberg, J. and Ahlberg A. (Reprinted 1991) *The Worm Book,* London: Armada Paperbacks.

Ahlberg, J. and Ahlberg, A. (1976) *The Old Joke Book*. London: Penguin Books.

Bird, M. (1984) *The Witch's Handbook*. NY: St Martin's Press.

Briggs, R. (1977) *Fungus the Bogeyman*. London: Hamish Hamilton.

Christie, P. (1986) 'Education in a school for autistic children' in *What's so special about autism?* Inge Wakehurst conference papers, National Autistic Society.

Collis, L. (1978) *Things We Say*. London: Thurman Publishing.

Snow, A. (1993) *How Dogs Really Work*. London: Harper Collins.

Terman, L. M. and Merrill, M. (1960) *Stanford-Binet Intelligence Scale*. Boston: Houghton Mifflin.

Webb, T. (1992) *A is For Autism* (video). London: Finetake Productions. Distributor: Connoisseur Video.

Chapter Nine

Conclusion: Towards a Pedagogy for Autism

Stuart Powell

Introduction

This chapter seeks to draw together some of the themes that have recurred throughout the chapters of this book. Its purpose is to begin to conceptualise a way of teaching and learning that is most likely to be effective in autism. It is important to stress that what follows is a collection of ideas that are derived from the practical examples, and the reflections upon them, provided by contributing authors to this book. This chapter does not claim to offer a definition of a pedagogy suitable for individuals with autism. Rather, it suggests that there are some common ideas in the way in which fellow authors go about their practical work in autism and that these may usefully be collected into a set of notions about how to establish an effective relationship between teaching, learning and autism. The collection of ideas is therefore the start of a 'bottom-up' approach to a notion of an effective pedagogy rather than a 'top-down' approach that might be based on an inclusive psychological description of learning needs in autism. In short, the sections below are not intended to be an exhaustive set of principles nor are they necessarily mutually exclusive – there are undoubtedly other equally significant aspects of any effective approach and some of the ideas expressed below do overlap.

Using the concrete, visual and spatial

Theo Peeters, in Chapter 2, points out that individuals with autism are relatively strong in processing information that is 'concrete, visible and spatial' but relatively weak in processing information that is abstract, invisible and temporal. The latter kinds of modality tend, in Peeters' words, to be both 'transient' and 'fugitive'. It may be hard for the non-autistic to fully appreciate just how powerful is the difference between the former and latter kinds of modality and just how difficult it becomes for the child with autism to learn when the teacher's style makes use almost exclusively of ways of behaving that are dependent on an understanding of the abstract (e.g. 'let's go out into the playground where you can *enjoy* yourself'), the invisible (e.g. 'do you *see what I mean*') and the temporal (e.g. 'if we wait a *little longer* the bus will come'). (Note that in the last of these examples I have interpreted Peeters literally in his use of 'temporal' in order to make the point as clear as possible. It should be noted that, in his conception, 'temporal' not only means about time but also about other information that is transient or fugitive rather than spatial.)

It does seem, then, that teachers need to try to devise ways of teaching that transform messages into concrete, visual and spatial modalities. This is not only a matter of avoiding certain ways of presenting information and communicating ideas but also of identifying the strengths that exist in these modalities and that therefore may be seen as strengths of an autistic way of thinking. For example, in a pedagogy for autism a picture may be worth a thousand words, even if it may seem to be harder to manage in a teaching and learning situation because it is not so readily available nor as flexible as the spoken word. Clearly, differing strengths in relation to the modalities noted do not just affect the delivery of the curriculum. The way in which the content of that curriculum is decided upon and organised is also a matter for concern in this respect (one needs to recognise here that in the UK at least decisions about curriculum are set in the context of a National Curriculum). To take a rather direct and blunt example, 'telling the time' is an aspect of schooling that may need a different place in the hierarchy of learning that can be expected of a child. It will also need an approach that recognises the potential of concrete ways of recording the passing of time and of, for example, the advantages of digital time display over analogue for someone who is relatively more comfortable with the clear visual identification of a number than the 'invisible' areas of a typical clock face.

- *Summary:* When planning the curriculum and its delivery teachers need to consider how best to make use of the strengths that an individual with autism may have in concrete, visible and spatial domains.

What goes on *between* teacher and learner

When discussing teaching and learning there may be a temptation to focus on one of the two participants – that is, on the teacher or on the learner. It is also tempting to see those roles as discrete with the teacher only teaching and the learner only learning. In Chapter 4 Melanie Nind points out the usefulness of focusing on what goes on *between* teacher and learner. Certainly in autism the boundaries between what it is to teach and what it is to learn break down. The teacher needs to conceptualise the act of teaching as engaging in a joint enterprise where what it is to learn is as important as ensuring that particular knowledge or skill has been learnt.

To follow as well as lead

The learning that is needed for an effective pedagogy in autism is one in which both individuals are learning about how to be effective interactors and learners with each other (see Nind this volume). Using the analogy of development within the social domain being a kind of dance: then both partners need to learn to move together if synchrony is to be achieved. The teacher needs, in one sense at least, to relinquish the element of control that typifies the 'normal' teaching and learning pattern – to follow as well as lead. It is not so much that one partner (the teacher) has the knowledge and needs simply to be willing and able to convey it to the other (the pupil), rather that the teacher needs to match the pace and direction of his/her abilities and expectations to those of the pupil. In Chapter 5, Wendy Prevezer shows how a teaching aim, to motivate and enable the child to use pre-verbal conversation skills, can be realised by following the child's agenda. Similarly, Flo Longhorn (Chapter 3) shows how an effective educative process can start usefully with a focus on the learner rather than with a set of prescribed educational aims. At a different level from either of these authors the teacher who wants to teach a child, for example, certain cookery skills needs to begin by considering those skills in relation to the child's likes and desires. Children with autism tend to like what they like (unaffected by the whims of others or the indicators of social acceptability) and will work and problem solve for their own ends. Developing knowledge and skills about cooking, in the first instance at least, will therefore be a manageable process when the attainment of those skills matches with the pupil's own agenda, i.e. accords with likes and dislikes.

The child as teacher

In autism, getting children to act as instructors may be a good way to enable them to focus on what they know for themselves. Golding (private correspondence) has found that children with autism can benefit greatly from role reversal in teaching and learning situations. That is, once a teacher has ensured that the child can do something, perhaps construct a model (or cross the road), then the child teaches a teacher (preferably a naïve stooge) how to perform the task. The act of teaching makes the child focus on their understanding of the task – they are required to make explicit the learning that needs to go on. Where possible the child, once successful at teaching the teacher, may go on to teach a peer. This approach moves away from the traditional teaching approach where the teacher has information, imparts it and then asks questions to check if the pupil knows the answers. This latter kind of directive teaching can become one where dependence rather than independence for the learner is likely to result and where dependence on rote memory will increase. For example, one of the difficulties that pupils with autism integrated into mainstream settings sometimes have is that they cannot see the point of retelling to the teacher what they know the teacher already knows (because the teacher told them in the first place).

- *Summary:* When analysing practice in order to improve the effectiveness of teaching and learning it may be useful to focus on what goes on *between* teacher and learner, to conceptualise the teacher as learner (of how the child can be enabled to learn) and to consider the possibilities of the learner as teacher (of how he/she understands).

Social and asocial learning

In this chapter I have made mention of the need to aim for a match between the teacher's way of teaching and the pupil's way of learning. I have also argued that recognising, as best we are able, the way the individual with autism thinks about the world is prerequisite for an effective pedagogy. The question arises then as to whether that match and that recognition require that the teacher adopt an autistic agenda and an autistic style; in short, if effective learning in autism is most likely to take place in what may be termed an autistic environment. Such an environment might, for example, involve a reduction in personal communication and an emphasis on heavily structured, concrete learning tasks; it would be a non-social environment. A resolution of this question may be derived from the content of what is to be learnt. Put simply: some, but not all, things may be most readily learnt by the pupil with autism in contexts where the social dimension to learning is reduced to a necessary minimum.

I should note at this point that much of the work described in this book focuses on the learning of social understanding and skills. For example, Melanie Nind argues that the best response to difficulty with social learning is to learn about the social world and about learning socially *through* social interaction. Tomas Tjus and Mikael Heimann describe the use of a computer-generated set of activities as the context for social interactions between teacher and pupil. Elizabeth Newson discusses the way in which social relationships can be facilitated by humour and form part of the therapeutic strand seen as necessary for successful education in autism. Despite this focus, in the introductory chapter I described an autistic way of thinking as essentially of an asocial kind where individuals are *in a psychological sense* outside of the social understandings that enable ready learning about socially defined things. In order to resolve the tension between pedagogic aims on the one hand and psychological states in autism on the other we may need to accommodate two apparently contradictory possibilities. First, that individuals with autism may learn some things most effectively in asocial contexts (e.g. learning about how a television works from a computer-based learning program). Second, that though such individuals may learn about how to be social in mechanistic ways (e.g. by having the rules of social behaviour set out for them in textual commentary on video sequences), they may learn the flexibility that is the distinguishing feature of social behaviour *only* when they are exposed to it and when opportunities are carefully constructed wherein they can experience it. An example of this might be in the use of Intensive Interaction as described by Melanie Nind (for further discussion of the issues raised here see Nind and Powell in press).

In short, children with autism may learn naturally in an asocial kind of way while teachers may teach naturally in a social kind of way. A new way clearly has to be found therefore in which teachers learn the implications of an autistic thinking style on learning potential and also learn how best to accommodate their own performance to match that potential. The teacher becomes first and foremost a learner about the way knowledge has been socially constructed and the way in which it is socially imparted. That teacher needs to ask how certain knowledge or skill can be made meaningful for children with autism in such a way as to give them control over it, and the way it can be used in future, related situations (i.e. how they can learn, know that they have learnt and learn to use what they have learnt).

Also, it is clear that a wholly asocial learning context may not be a realistic possibility in the classroom (even if it were deemed to be a desirable aim). Tomas Tjus and Mikael Heimann (Chapter 7) show how the way in which the teacher acts within the triad of child, teacher and computer material is significant for the effectiveness of learning. They give the example of the development of joint attention in relation to verbal exposure, and show how the computer can be made to act as a facilitating mediator which circumvents the usual need to employ head and eye movements and vocalisations as referential cues towards joint attention to objects (this being problematic for the individual with autism). Computers may be extremely useful in controlling learning environments to the autistic learner's advantage but this is not to imply their use in isolation of social input at the levels of curriculum design and delivery.

Certainly it may well be, as Tjus and Heimann suggest, that increasing the relevant information and decreasing the irrelevant information may facilitate processing in working memory. Multimedia representations and socially delivered recasts may allow 'rich connections' between representations of the same meaning in different modes in such a way as to avoid what would in the normal course of events be a heavy burden on working memory. What is interesting here is the combination of social and non-social inputs.

Readers may wish to refer to the chapter by Wendy Prevezer (Chapter 5) where there is discussion of possible difficulties in asocial teaching methods.

- *Summary:* The way in which learning is, typically, socially contrived is not necessarily amenable to the way in which children with autism think and learn. A special accommodation may therefore be necessary in which some information and skills may be presented in asocial contexts and where special attention is always paid to the social relationships within any teaching and learning situation. But it is also the case that learning to be social will effectively take place within a social relationship or, conceivably, within a context in which social relationships are accurately modelled.

Learning to 'tune in' to the pupil with autism

In Chapter 8 Elizabeth Newson writes, 'obviously we have only been able to do this by managing to tune in to them'. In the chapters by Flo Longhorn and by

Wendy Prevezer there is a strong sense of these authors waiting patiently and catching the moment when progress can be made. Indeed Wendy Prevezer talks quite directly about her contributions to the kind of 'pre-verbal conversation' needing to be 'finely tuned'. Reflection on your own practice with children with autism may indicate that moments come in the ebb and flow of activities and actions when you are able to 'tune in' to the child. Perhaps these are moments of communication in an otherwise non-communicative relationship, perhaps they are moments when 'power and control' within the teacher–pupil relationship are shared (see Wendy Prevezer Chapter 5), and perhaps they are a matter of serendipity as much as planning. One can argue of course that such moments are features of teaching generally and while this may well be the case it is probably also true that these moments are less frequent and more elusive in autism and therefore more significant when they do occur. Whatever the case, it does seem that in autism the moment when teacher and pupil are tuned in together is something that teachers can come to recognise and utilise with time and experience. It is not necessarily a concept that is amenable to scientific description let alone identification and measurement but this does not mean that it lacks power and significance. Elizabeth Newson shows that it is possible to *learn* how to tune in to the child. This is achieved by careful observation, control of one's own responses and imaginative structuring of tasks.

In a wider sense Harry Procter (Chapter 6) shows how it is possible for the teacher or therapist to use an understanding of personal constructs to learn about the specific mechanisms operating within, in this case, a family's relationships. This is then part of the 'careful observation' noted above; it enables the therapist to tune in to how the family is functioning and therefore to determine what is likely to be a productive intervention. Further, the use of personal constructs is seen as a way of getting family members to understand better their own place in the interactions taking place. In this way such constructs enable those family members to tune in to their own situation ('the discourse of sociality is encouraged and introduced into the family's daily life').

- *Summary:* In autism, moments when pupil and teacher are 'in tune' may be few and far between but when they arrive they need to be effectively used. Teachers need to learn both patience and ways of tuning in to how their pupils with autism are thinking and feeling. To do this requires more than being sensitive to the kinds of things that are usually indicative of mood; it requires learning about the idiosyncratic and complex indicators that relate to the particular individual concerned.

Needing to establish mutuality

In many of the chapters in this book the potential of mutuality within the teaching and learning process is explored. For example Melanie Nind describes the achievement of mutual pleasure as being central to Intensive Interaction, Flo Longhorn discusses a meaningful relationship being developed at the level of mutual sensations and Wendy Prevezer notes the importance of moments of 'give and take' during musical interaction. Similarly, Harry Procter argues for the conversation that goes on within a therapy session as the way in which mutual understanding can be developed within the family (i.e. when individuals begin to negotiate the meaning of their experiences with others).

If a teaching and learning episode in autism does not engender mutuality (whether that be of sensation, fun or understanding) then it is not likely to lead to learning that is meaningful, flexible and ultimately generalisable. The individual with autism needs to be shown not just that information can be learned but also that it can be shared. It is when the individual is able to understand that things can mean different things to different people, and subsequently what certain things may mean to others as well as to themselves, that they are in a position to be able to negotiate meaning. Indeed, many of the examples of practice given by contributing authors indicate that establishing mutuality is a prerequisite for this kind development.

- *Summary:* Teaching and learning situations need to be analysed for ways in which mutuality of experience and hence understanding can be developed. Teachers need to think through how their pupils with autism can be enabled to share their understanding with others as a precursor to developing an awareness of 'negotiated meaning'. For example, the child might 'teach' a stooge how to solve a particular puzzle with which they themselves are wholly familiar or draw a map to enable a peer to find their way to a 'treasure'.

Enabling those with autism to progress from self-regulation to independent thinking

For many of the contributing authors to this book the matter of education is inseparable from the aim of engendering independent thinking in their pupils. The starting place for this aim may be in seeking to 'intellectually and emotionally arouse the child and to enable the child to learn to self-regulate this arousal' (Nind, this volume). Whether the medium is music or computers or joke telling authors equate 'progress' with increased self-determination.

One danger of teaching individuals with autism is that of being drawn in to a downward spiral of: pupil dependency – increasing teacher ability to help the pupil to cope – increasing pupil dependency on that ability. As a response to this danger some of the authors in this book have shown how independence must be respected at whatever level the child is able to operate and nurtured whenever appropriate. For example Natalie's ability to state her feelings and assert her intentions by putting on a large pair of boots to preclude communication via the soles of the feet is interpreted by Flo Longhorn as a clear sign of the establishment of a relationship. Longhorn's reaction as a teacher is to acknowledge and accept. This of course gives power to the gesture and thus initiates learning on the part of Natalie ('I can control this person in this situation').

At a different level Theo Peeters, in his chapter, describes ways of organising the physical environment so that particular behaviours and activities are associated (in the mind of the pupil with autism) with predictable places. The result of such organisation is that life for the individual pupil is 'a little bit more under control', he/she will have gained a 'bit of power and independence'. Here it is what the pupil feels, or understands to be the case, that matters rather than the amount of manipulation of circumstances by the teacher.

- *Summary:* If self-regulation can be established at whatever level is appropriate for the individual pupil then that pupil is in a position to progress towards independent thinking. The rhythm of music, the 'dance' of social interaction, the redesigning of a joke or the organisation of the room: all are contexts within which the pupil can learn to recognise then regulate their own responses. Such learning is a first step towards being able to act independently.

Using the senses in learning

Flo Longhorn (this volume) writes persuasively about how the senses may be used to 'breach the barrier into the world of special people and form a platform from which to go forward together in their education'. Certainly it does seem that in autism we need to rethink the relationship between the five senses and learning. In non-autistic development using sensation to learn tends to be a stage on the way to learning about the world through the social media of language and visual representation. Children in school learn about the five senses but not necessarily through them. In autism, however, it seems that sensation persists as a meaningful route to understanding beyond the stage of mental development where it is normally relegated to the status of a less than efficient way of finding out about the world (except of course in particular domains). The 11-year-old child with autism who persists in 'tasting' new people he encounters is acting in what is for him a problem-solving, information seeking way. There may be all sorts of legitimate reasons to want to move him on to other ways of problem-solving in this context but teachers need to recognise that this kind of tasting may be working (in the sense of enabling understanding) for this individual. Therefore to take away the behaviour without giving the child some other way of gaining the necessary information would be to deny a learning opportunity. There are clearly difficult ethical and practical issues surrounding this area. Using a taste in a learning programme without knowing whether it may provoke sensuality or nausea (to take two of the possibilities from Figure 3.2) is clearly problematic. Nevertheless, using the potential of all five senses as a 'sensory framework for a more formal education' (Longhorn, this volume) may well be a necessary pedagogic strategy for many individuals with autism and a useful one for others. Wendy Prevezer illustrates a similar point in her work with sounds combined with physical movement and contact and strong visual messages.

Theo Peeters makes the point that teachers are sometimes too keen to move children on to the next level of learning and understanding when, in fact, a child may need to continue to gain in real learning at the level at which he/she has proved operationally effective. If that level involves the senses then potentials in this respect need to be explored.

- *Summary:* In autism we need to recognise that effective learning may take place through all five of the senses. Such learning should not be under-estimated and certainly it may provide a sound basis for moving forward to other more conceptually-based education.

Continuous evaluation of the teaching and learning process

It is clear from reading all of the contributing authors to this book that an ability to monitor the process of teaching and learning in an ongoing and evaluative way is seen as crucial to a teacher's effectiveness. Of course, such monitoring may be seen as an essential component of teaching in the most general sense with all children regardless of whether or not they are autistic. And clearly it is the case that effective teaching, wherever it exists, requires that teachers monitor the on-going effects of their words and actions on pupils' learning. But in autism that monitoring may need to be of a qualitatively different kind. Here the teacher needs to evaluate in terms of a whole range of possible origins of pupil actions and words that may be unrelated to the context, aims or content of the teaching. This evaluation will not necessarily be in terms of how the child appears to be learning or not learning in the conventional sense, e.g. responding to questions in such a way as to indicate understanding. Particular words uttered by the teacher may trigger specific memories in the child with autism, which bear no apparent relationship to the current situation. The teacher needs to recognise the power of these memories *for the child* rather than dismiss them as unrelated and irrelevant.

Harry Procter (Chapter 6) offers a systemic approach to analysing ongoing interactions. He points out that for an evaluation of what is happening in a teaching and learning situation to be effective requires that it take into account the actions and reactions of all the players in any social scenario. One can only understand a child's words, actions or behaviours in relation to the context and to the words, actions and behaviours of others. Monitoring in this sense needs to involve an analysis of the various constructs that interplay. Importantly, and distinctively, in autism this analysis needs to take into account a notion of the individual as having constructs that are not organised in the usual 'hierarchical' way (see Procter this volume), but are fragmented into idiosyncratic, unrelated meanings and that do not readily subsume other people's constructs. Therefore the ongoing monitoring by teachers of children with autism needs to recognise that the usually accepted constructing and reconstructing of meaning and relationships may be disrupted. For example, where one normally accepts that the response of peers to a particular activity such as listening to a story will affect the individual learner one way or the other, this cannot necessarily be accepted in autism. In this case the construct of 'listening to a story' may, for example, involve a need to wear a particular item of clothing and will not necessarily take account of other children's apparent pleasure or displeasure, listening behaviour and so on.

Melanie Nind (Chapter 4) discusses the need for an enhanced level of reflection as part of the ongoing monitoring of a learning episode. For example, she discusses responding to the child *as if* that child had intended, and so highlighting that intention is possible and indicating what can be achieved. She recognises that this is problematic in autism but argues that 'the natural pedagogy is powerful and can be made even more powerful by augmenting it with layers of reflection'. Her argument for an effective pedagogy revolves around a combining of intuitive responding with careful reflection. Clearly, in Intensive Interaction what teachers do will be contingent on the actions of the child. As well as suggesting following the child's lead Nind argues for continual observation and the interpretation of non-verbal feedback in such a way as to enable 'micro-adjustments' and ultimately 'optimum levels of attention and arousal'.

It has been argued elsewhere (Powell and Jordan 1993) that teacher reflection in autism needs, on occasion, to be counter intuitive. The kinds of interpretations that can be made legitimately when reflecting on teaching and learning with non-autistic children may not be sustained in autism. The opening chapter of this volume sets out the basis for this argument. Certainly when teachers reflect on the usefulness of things such as further, different verbal explanation or close physical proximity as a way of encouragement, then it becomes clear that the normal interpretive template for behaviour and learning needs restructuring. In short, when intuition follows the normally developing template it may mislead rather than inform.

- *Summary:* Effective teaching of individuals with autism requires a particular form of ongoing evaluation which involves a high level of reflection and takes account of the idiosyncratic nature of learning in autism. It may involve counter intuitive thinking on the part of the teacher.

The distinction between teaching and learning

Clearly, the act of teaching is distinct from the act of learning. Many of the chapters in this book have described intricate relationships between what teachers do when they teach and what those with autism receive when they learn, and some authors have argued for particular attention to be paid to what goes on between teacher and learner – the interactive process. But it is also the case that while we may say that all things that can be taught can also be learnt it is not similarly the case that all things that can be learnt can be taught. I may learn to love someone or something but this does not mean that I can teach someone else to love in these ways. Children may learn to recognise their mother's voice and may learn what their mother means when she looks towards an object but these things are not necessarily teachable.

In autism we have to accept that some things may simply not be teachable – yet it would not necessarily be true that these same things might not be learnable by the individual with autism. Indeed it might be argued that while children with autism are not amenable to being taught they may nevertheless be quite able to learn. Educators are in danger of interpreting the act of learning as being inexorably linked with a prerequisite act of teaching. It would be erroneous to say 'this child cannot engage in problem solving because he does not respond to any of my ways of teaching problem solving', when that same child is able to locate a chair of the necessary height to stand upon in order to reach the appropriate key from a large selection, in order to open the door to a 'forbidden' room which in turn allows access to an outdoor play area. Clearly, in this instance the child has learnt by application of problem-solving strategies, involving observation and estimation at the very least, how to solve the problem of gaining access to the play area.

Melanie Nind (this volume) makes clear the dangers of trying to break down into small, distinct steps that can be taught what is normally learnt without apparent effort. For example, a teacher may painstakingly break down sandwich making into small, discrete, teachable steps and 'successfully' teach each step. But it does not follow that the pupil will have learnt how to make a sandwich. Indeed, in autism, the teacher is likely to have taught the pupil to be dependent on cues being given as to the nature, duration and order of the sequence of activities that make up sandwich making. It is quite likely that without the appropriate cues at the right moments the child will simply continue to butter the bread or spread the jam until rescued by the cue-giving, 'successful' teacher.

Thus it becomes necessary for teachers to think not only about how they can usefully teach things but also how best they can organise a context that is conducive to learning without requiring input of an instructional or interventionist kind. In her chapter Elizabeth Newson discusses ways in which children have been enabled to learn about humour and how to manipulate and use it. She illustrates that it is possible to enable children with autism to think flexibly. The 'other-way-round world' that she creates with James, and which he takes on to new heights of absurdity by pursuing the logicality of what would follow if certain premises are accepted, is a context in which James is enabled to demonstrate that he can think flexibly. One could argue of course that James is really only pursuing the logic of his new, reversed world – that his rigidity of thought persists, albeit within a new and different set of circumstances and constraints. But this would be to miss the point. What has happened is that the 'other-way-round world' is the context within which he is able to be in a position to amuse other people. Thus he has the experience of being funny and of making people laugh. Humour and what it is to be humorous can, in this way, be learned. Similarly, the further goal of flexible thought is attainable in as much as James is now able to take a set of givens (the way the world is) and imagine what would happen if they changed. Just because we know of his inherent difficulties with flexible thinking we should not be blinded to the fact that he has achieved flexible thought. Those who think that pursuing logicalities when the givens change while other things remain constant (so cats begin to bark while retaining their other feline characteristics) is not really imaginative and funny at all might usefully reflect on the works of Lewis Carroll or Salvador Dali.

- *Summary:* It is useful in autism to focus on the differences between teaching and learning (as well as upon the interactions between them). It may be the case that those with autism can learn (as is evidenced by their behaviour in non-academic settings) but may not be receptive to being taught. It follows from this that teachers might usefully conceptualise their task as being one of finding ways of enabling learning rather than of organising teaching.

Interpreting the child with autism as a successful learner

The child with autism may present various complex and in many cases apparently extreme challenges for the educator and there may be a tendency to focus on all the things that the child cannot do or does not seem to be able to do effectively (and perhaps to feel overwhelmed by them). While this is understandable at one level it may be unproductive at another. Flo Longhorn (Chapter 3) discusses the need to 'ascertain her [Natalie's] established self-taught activities'. It is important to take on the perspective that many of the things that Natalie could do had been self-taught. Again, these things need to be seen first and foremost as examples of learning (regardless for the moment of their social or personal implications – though clearly such implications may need consideration as part of a separate and equally legitimate agenda). An analysis of just what the child can do and the kind of experiences that have led to that learning may be useful starting points for the teacher. In short, the teacher needs to conceptualise the child as a successful learner (at whatever level that may be and however tenuous that notion of success is) with potential for further learning rather than as an evident non-performer or weak performer. It is perhaps important to stress here that, again, I am taking an interpretation of learning that goes beyond what might typically be thought of as school or academic learning.

- *Summary:* The teacher needs to analyse what the child can do and has learnt in such a way as to focus on the learning that has been achieved, how it has come about and what it reveals about the child's potential for further learning.

Teachers behaving predictably

Teachers' attention is often drawn to ways in which the environment can be modified or controlled so as to enable the individual with autism to function more effectively (see, for example, Peeters this volume). It is also the case, of course, that the teacher can modify or control his/her own way of behaving so as to better enable learning on the part of the individual. Again, there is a sense in which this is a commonplace feature of all teaching. But in autism there is a need for teachers to focus on one dimension of their behaviour and make themselves more predictable so that the demands on the individual pupil are reduced. Wendy Prevezer quotes from Jolliffe *et al.* (1992) to show how much demand is placed by human beings who move unexpectedly and make varying noises and so on. Prevezer sees it as part of the teacher's challenge to behave predictably enough for

Tina to make sense of actions, gestures, sounds and words. Clearly, she uses music as a structure for that predictability where others use different means (Melanie Nind for example uses, in part, responsive body movements). However predictability is achieved its importance for the learner with autism is significant. Teachers who are successful in teaching children with autism are often those who either knowingly or unknowingly have learnt to become more predictable for their pupils. It is important to note that predictability here is not necessarily synonymous with lack of excitement or lack of change. Children with autism can respond well to excitement and change but they need to be able to determine when and how those things are going to occur. Peeters (1997) gives the example of the child who throws a tantrum at Christmas time because he cannot cope with being given a surprise present. When he is taught about the present that will come and instructed as to the nature and timing of its arrival then he is able to look forward to the present and enjoy the 'surprise' when it happens. Readers may wonder if this does not imply that the real surprise has been forsaken. Again this is to impose a non-autistic agenda on the situation. If the point of the present giving is to give pleasure then that has been achieved – if the child is enabled to learn about present receiving then this is an additional gain.

Establishing predictability could, of course, be counter productive to the overall aim of increasing independence of thought if it led to a situation where teacher and pupil began to engage in a kind of joint ritual extended across times and places. As already noted, change can still be a part of the consistent environment and of relationships within it. The need for predictability should not be allowed to become an excuse for lack of change but rather should be the framework within which change is planned for and encouraged. See Wendy Prevezer (this volume) for examples of ways of being flexible within the boundaries of the individual with autism's need for predictability.

- *Summary:* Children with autism need a predictable and ordered environment if they are to learn effectively. The teacher's behaviour is a significant aspect of this and teachers therefore need to strive for the kind of consistency that avoids disruption to patterns of actions and subsequent confusion for the pupil with autism.

Conclusion

The first chapter in this book ended with a consideration of some words from Jim Sinclair (1992). On re-reading those words in the context of the intervening, contributory chapters I am struck, again, by the awesome effort to learn about the world that is made by many individuals with autism – by Natalie for example. Sinclair asks, 'Work with me to build bridges between us.' This seems the very least we can do. Those who are not autistic have the advantage of being insiders in the game of generating and sustaining shared social meaning. Those with autism, on the other hand, are outside of the game looking in. In this sense the non-autistic are the 'stronger' of the partners in any kind of joint venture as desired by Sinclair.

Theo Peeters points out in his chapter that, 'the strong should adapt to the weaker, not the other way round'. This present chapter describes an approach to a pedagogy for autism that seeks partnership in bridge building and which acknowledges both the starting point of our partners with autism and the efforts they make in trying to connect. It argues for adaptation to the ways and needs of those with autism and further for a kind of adaptation that permeates both curriculum design and teaching approach. To create an effective pedagogy for autism requires a fundamental re-appraisal of what those of us without autism have tended to conceptualise as *the* process of teaching and learning.

Acknowledgement

I am grateful to the contributing authors who commented upon an early draft of this chapter. Their responses to my use of their ideas and words were invaluable.

References

Golding (1999) private correspondence

Jolliffe, T., Lansdowne, R. and Robinson, C. (1992) 'Autism: a personal account', *Communication* **26**(3).

Nind, M. and Powell, S. D. (in press) 'Intensive interaction and autism: some theoretical concerns,' *Children and Society*.

Peeters, T. (1997) *Autism: from theoretical understanding to educational intervention*. London: Whurr Publishers.

Powell, S. D. and Jordan, R. R. (1993) 'Diagnosis, intuition and autism', *British Journal of Special Education* **20**(1), 26–9.

Sinclair, J. (1992) 'Bridging the gaps: an inside-out view of autism', in Schopler, E. and Mesibov, G. (eds) *High Functioning Individuals with Autism*. New York: Plenum Press.

Index